About the aut

NATASHA HOFFMAN has a degree in Fine Art. For twenty years she taught art and design at Hastings Art College, England, at the same time bringing up her four children. From an early age she was aware of a heightened intuitive ability, and wanting to work in a more personal way with people, she gave up teaching to study various methods of Energy Healing. Since then she has worked with both individuals and the environment, aiming to restore balance and harmony. Honed over the last twenty years, her intuitive skills have broadened, leading her to the Carnac megaliths and the inspirational messages held in them, which became the subject of her first book. In addition to her writing and healing work, Natasha is still a practicing artist and continues to sell her work in England and France.

Her partner **Hamilton Hill** graduated from Oxford University with an MA in history. For twenty-five years he lived and worked in London as a consultant in commercial real estate. Moving in 1976 to the beautiful Sussex countryside with his family—he has three children—he worked a 200-acre farm run on organic principles until retirement.

Natasha and he divide their time between Dartmouth, England, and the Auvergne in France, where they have restored an old farmhouse. They are members of the British Society of Dowsers.

CAROLYN NORTH works as an energy healer who uses movement and sound. She has written nine books that explore, in memoir form, the intersection of matter and spirit.

She and her husband were members of the Findhorn-inspired community, Shenoa, in Northern California, where she designed the community's mandala garden and they built the world's first Permitted rice-strawbale house. She considers herself to be a social activist who uses innovative arts and meditative practice as ways to promote the expansion of consciousness, and she takes great pleasure in all the different forms it takes.

She lives in Berkeley, California, with her husband and has three married children, four grandchildren, and two god-grandchildren.

(www.healingimprovisations.net)

green press INITIATIVE

Findhorn Press is committed to preserving ancient forests and natural resources. We elected to print this title on 30% post consumer recycled paper, processed chlorine free. As a result, for this printing, we have saved:

7 Trees (40' tall and 6-8" diameter)
2 Million BTUs of Total Energy
660 Pounds of Greenhouse Gases
3,179 Gallons of Wastewater
193 Pounds of Solid Waste

Findhorn Press made this paper choice because our printer, Thomson-Shore, Inc., is a member of Green Press Initiative, a nonprofit program dedicated to supporting authors, publishers, and suppliers in their efforts to reduce their use of fiber obtained from endangered forests.

For more information, visit www.greenpressinitiative.org

Environmental impact estimates were made using the Environmental Defense Paper Calculator. For more information visit: www.papercalculator.org.

Voices Out of Stone

Other books by **Carolyn North**

Ecstatic Relations

Seven Movements, One Song

The Experience of a Lifetime

The Musicians and the Servants

Other book by **Natasha Hoffman**

Let the Standing Stones Speak

Voices Out of Stone

Magic and Mystery in Megalithic Brittany

Carolyn North
&
Natasha Hoffman

Illustrations by Natasha Hoffman

With a Foreword and
Afterword by Hamilton Hill

FINDHORN PRESS

Published in 2010 by Findhorn Press, Scotland

ISBN 978-1-84409-195-9

A CIP record for this title is available from the British Library.

Edited by Nicky Leach
Cover design by Sara Glaser
Cover photograph by Corson Hirshfeld
Interior design and maps by Damian Keenan

Printed and bound in the USA

1 2 3 4 5 6 7 8 9 17 16 15 14 13 12 11 10

Published by

Findhorn Press

117-121 High Street,

Forres IV36 1AB,

Scotland, UK

t +44 (0)1309 690582

f +44 (0)131 777 2711

e info@findhornpress.com

www.findhornpress.com

Contents

Contents

Contents

DEDICATION

To M.W. somewhere in the world

SPECIAL THANKS to Hamilton Hill and Herb Strauss for being there, again and again, when we needed them.

FOREWORD

Hamilton Hill

TWO PEOPLE—a single, shared vision of another world. This book recounts the experiences of two women at the same place in France, some ten years apart, written down without consultation and mostly before they even came to know each other. One is American, the other English, and each has several children. They share a common language and Jewish ancestry, but above all they have both had the singular privilege of receiving information and guidance—channeled messages in the mind, if you like—as direct communication from a spiritual source.

The place is Carnac on the Brittany coast, the well-known World Heritage Site of the megalithic era, where thousands of standing stones may still be seen in their extended and impressive alignments. It seems that these ancient stones have a form of memory; they can hold information and act as a medium for its reception by a human being. It's much like gaining access to the storage capacity of a computer. We may know it works but not understand why, nor how to retrieve the information.

The authors have the password. There is no reason to doubt that these are genuine experiences—their force, simplicity, and similarity are convincing enough. The question for most people will be who or what inspired them? Where do they originate? A rational explanation, deemed necessary by today's science and medicine, may evade us. It would probably not have been sought at all by the philosophers of ancient Greece, nor by the sages of traditional Eastern philosophies, who did not analyze. They accepted mystical experience and inspiration, gods and Devic presences, as an integral part of life. For them, direct spiritual experience was just as real as what we usually call reality.

We know now that physical things are only real for us in terms of our limited sense perceptions. We don't need science to tell us that many of our cherished beliefs are local illusions, that with all our ceaseless, antlike, seemingly important activities, humanity is but a tiny part of a vast, highly organized, and unified Universe—a network of frequencies and energy fields about which we really know very little.

In this book, we are told of direct experiences from an other-than-human level. One person might think of these experiences as disembodied cosmic energy, a parallel to our embodied form of earthly energy; another might call them Angelic, using the traditional name for a nonphysical being, a messenger of divine origin. We lack the necessary language for these manifestations of what is sometimes known as "subtle energy."

Each author has her own view on this, but leaves us free to choose for ourselves how we identify these energetic manifestations, in accordance with our own beliefs. Goethe used the term "Providence"; Jung spoke of the "Collective Unconscious." Today, many of us would regard it as communication with a vibrational field of universal consciousness, in which all things are recorded, and of which we human beings are an inseparable part.

Voices Out of Stone brings much-needed lightness, balance, and feminine intuition into an uneasy world, much of which has not yet outgrown masculine dominance, has scarcely even emerged from the aggressive power struggles of all our recorded history, and remains reluctant to acknowledge the reality of a spiritual realm. Such things may be changing; nothing is static. Those of us who feel that we are still living in dark times may remind ourselves that the deepest darkness always comes before the dawn. The Greek poet George Seferis, inspired by the ruins of ancient Mycenae, wrote:

Voices out of stone, out of sleep,
Voices more deep here,
where the world grows dark…

If our present societies are to avoid a similar collapse we have to change. We need to balance material demands and desires with spiritual awareness, to lift all our relationships to a higher and more loving plane. This is a book that can go with us on that journey toward a higher level of consciousness. It is not an easy path, but each one of us must take it if humanity is to survive.

Hamilton Hill
Boudy, France, 2008.

List of Illustrations

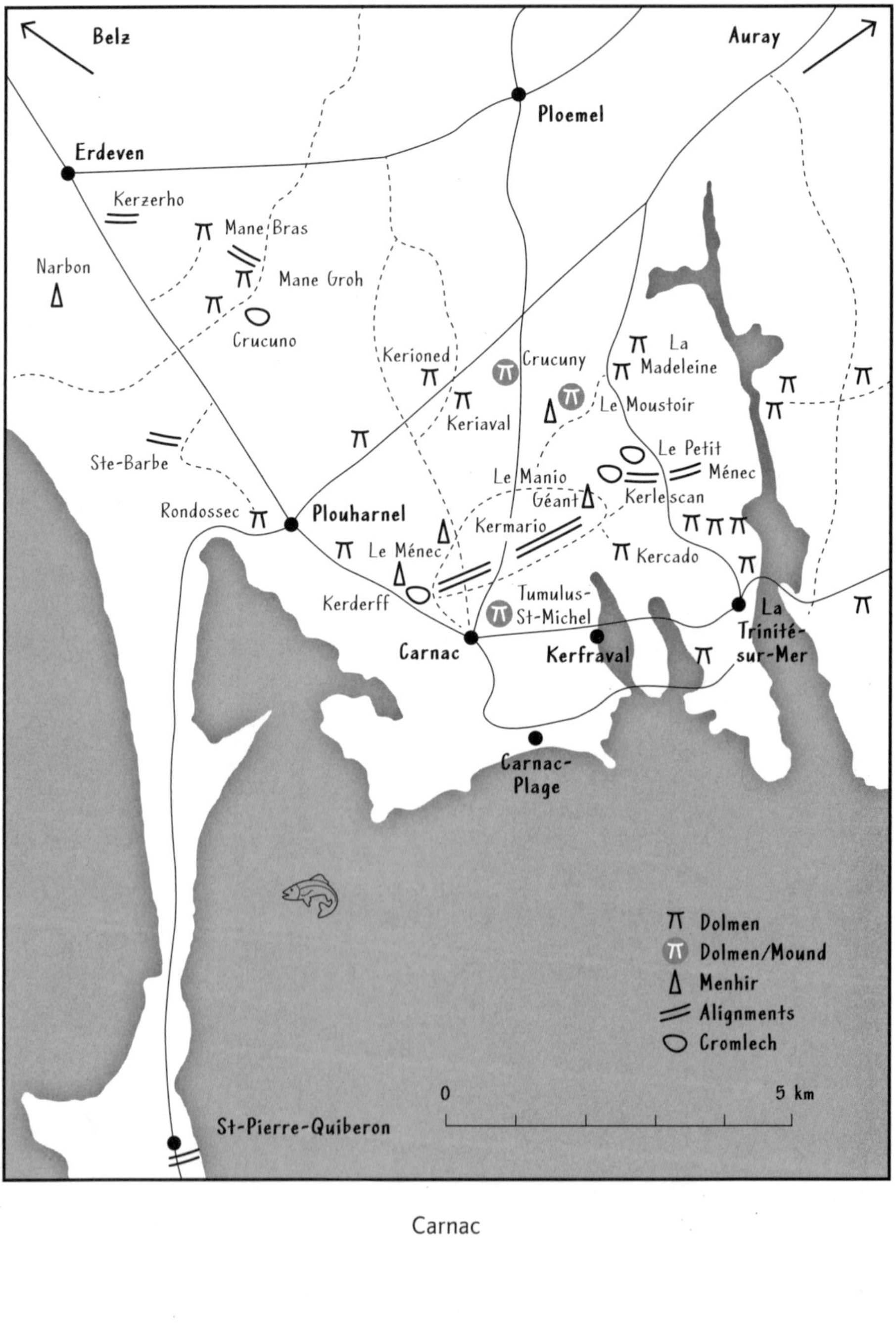
Belz
Auray
Ploemel
Erdeven
Kerzerho
Mane Bras
Narbon
Mane Groh
Crucuno
Kerioned
Crucuny
La Madeleine
Le Moustoir
Keriaval
Ste-Barbe
Le Petit Ménec
Le Manio
Géant
Kerlescan
Rondossec
Plouharnel
Kermario
Le Ménec
Kercado
Kerderff
Tumulus-St-Michel
La Trinité-sur-Mer
Carnac
Kerfraval
Carnac-Plage
Dolmen
Dolmen/Mound
Menhir
Alignments
Cromlech
0
5 km
St-Pierre-Quiberon

Carnac

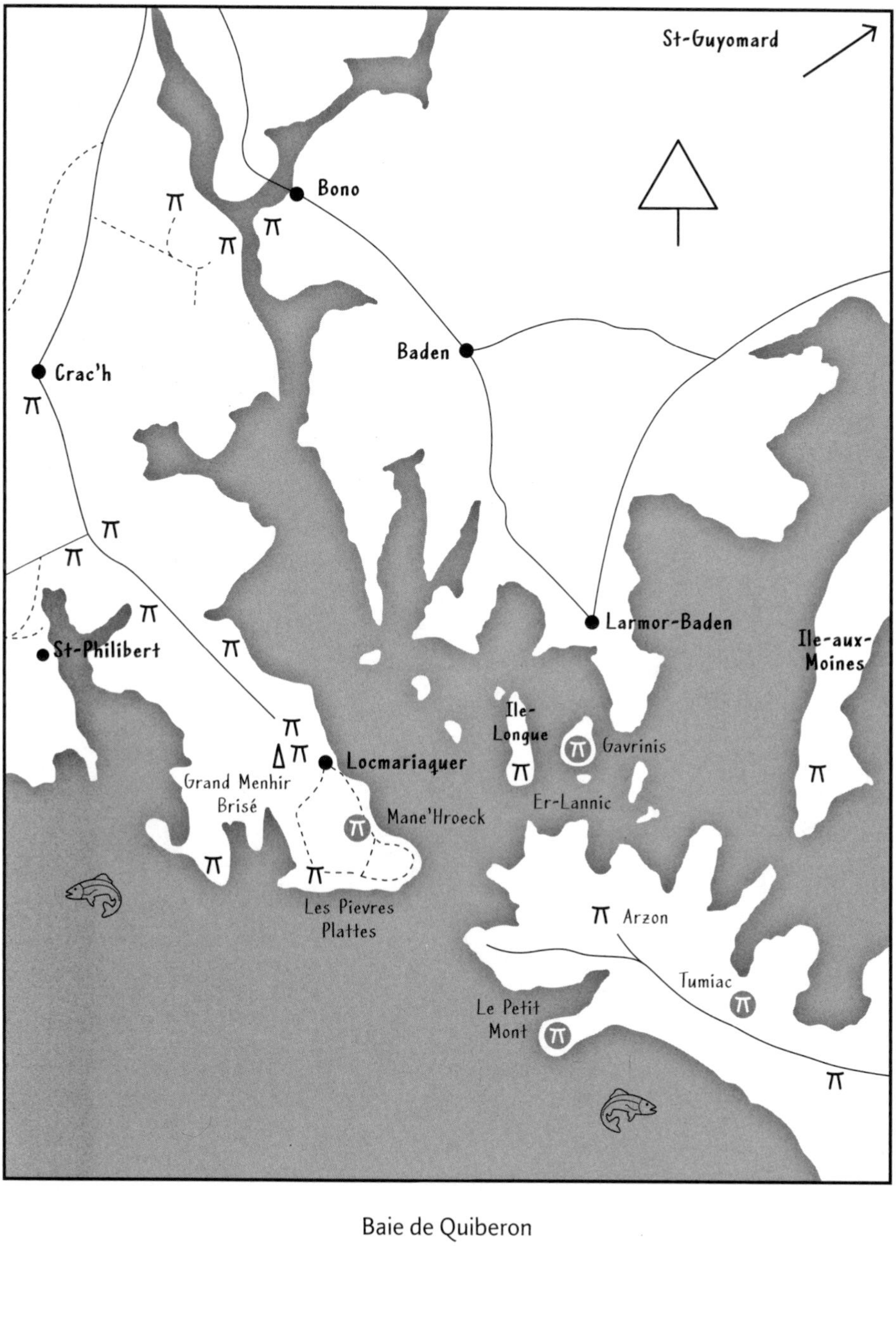

Baie de Quiberon

Author Introductions

Carolyn: A Picture in a Book

IN THE SUMMER OF 1984—my forty-fifth year and the year George Orwell made famous—I went on pilgrimage to the megaliths at Carnac. Until that time, I was a housewife living with my husband, a university scientist, and our three teenagers in Berkeley, California, fascinated by earth mysteries and indigenous belief systems, but quite content to stay at home reading whatever books I could find on the subjects.

The traveling we did in those days was done as a family, and I had no particular desire to travel alone. But when I saw this one haunting photograph of a chambered passage-mound in Brittany, in a pine forest with a standing stone on top, I felt drawn to go there. For reasons I could not fathom, it was familiar to me. Although I had never even been to that part of France, I somehow *knew* this particular place. It was called Kercado.

What was so fascinating to me about megaliths—stone circles, passage mounds, dolmens (stone chambers), menhirs (standing stones), and alignments—was that they could be found everywhere in the world, they predated written history, and were totally mysterious. Nobody, even the archaeologists, seemed to know who had put them there, nor how they managed to do so. Some modern experimenters have succeeded, using many strong men and log rollers, to lift huge stones but none have been able to carry them any distance. Even so, nobody understands why the people of that time had considered it important enough to make such a prodigious effort, however it was done!

When I first saw that photograph of Kercado and felt it call to me, I had another strong "knowing": that I must invite a particular person to come to Brittany with me—a young Czech guy I had once known but had not seen in almost ten years. I rarely even corresponded with Jiri, a scientist living and working in Switzerland, probably in his mid-thirties by now, but during the short period we had known each other in California our connection had been strong. So despite the strangeness of it I took a chance and contacted him, suggesting we meet in Brittany for the summer solstice. He was surprised to hear from me, but he agreed to come. As it happened, the reason for our making this trip together was revealed once we got there.

Those three weeks at the stones—one week in his company and two weeks on my own—turned out to be life changing for me. The stones became my teachers. What I mean by this is that I received messages from the stones; not that they "spoke" to me, exactly, but that I "heard" them with my mind's ears. Words would suddenly appear in my head, as would sudden insights, questions, instructions. In my mind's eye I seemed to "see" things, often multidimensional images I could feel as well as see. One day's teachings would prepare me for another day's teachings, and sometimes I would be told to stop altogether and just rest.

The messages were always caring, sometimes tough, and often humorous, as if whatever intelligence was guiding me cared greatly for my wellbeing. I was led, step by step, to revelations about the nature of the world. I was encouraged to experience all the intense emotions—grief, anger, love. I was allowed to make mistakes and learn from them. I kept a detailed journal of everything I experienced, and that journal is the basis for what I have written here.

A dolmen near Carnac

I was being taught how to listen closely and prepare my body and mind for the subtle information that was being transmitted. My whole being became a channel for these teachings. To this day I have no idea where this wise guidance came from, but it was at the stones in Brittany that I first experienced it, and it has informed my life and work ever since.

I have discovered that when I am able to be quiet and focused enough I can hear the teachings wherever I am, so I expect that all of us can have similar access to this same field of wisdom. At the stones I was shown the way, but I do not think we require ancient stones to hear what the Universe has to say. Needless to say, even though I have used what I learned there as the basis for much of my ongoing research, I rarely mention to people where my ideas come from. "Talking stones" would not go over very well with many of the people I know, so I have kept my own counsel and just carried on.

Then, in 2005, I discovered *Let The Standing Stones Speak* by Natasha Hoffman and Hamilton Hill in a local bookstore and read this beautiful and inspiring book in a single sitting. I grew more astonished at each turn of the page. Twenty-one years after my first trip to Carnac, I discovered that others had had similar experiences to mine at the same stones! Not only did many aspects of our stories match but so did much of the basic information we had received. Even more, what they learned seemed to update my experiences, making the guidance even more relevant to our increasingly treacherous times. I could hardly believe my luck.

Believe it, was what I heard.

Tracking down Natasha and Hamilton was not simple. We live on different continents, and it took me several months of consulting publishers and Internet telephone directories before I finally sent out stamped letters to every person by the name of Hoffman or Hill in Devon, England. I determined that if I got no response I would do the same in France. Luckily, one of those letters reached them and the connection was made.

We decided to co-write this book, telling our individual stories, continuing the dialogue with each other, and listening for guidance from wheresoever it comes. Whoever or whatever is speaking to us is adamant that we pass on the information we are receiving. We do so with great gratitude to our teachers and the shared pleasure of having found each other in the world.

Natasha: The Picture on a Biscuit Tin

I WAS BORN IN A SMALL VILLAGE in Wiltshire, England, not far from the famous megaliths at Stonehenge and Avebury—my mother often walked me around the stones when I was a baby. There were no fences and access was easy in those days, but not many people bothered to visit what may be the most important, and certainly among the most imposing, prehistoric sites in northern Europe. Little did she know it then, but my mother was in fact introducing me to the Old Ones, to a greater consciousness, linking me to an awareness of the past that I would later be able to tap.

That was my introduction, perhaps an initiation also, to the great stones left for us by our ancestors. Later on, first Carolyn, and ten years later, Hamilton and I, came to experience another vast arrangement of standing stones, this time in France: the alignments and dolmens of Carnac in Brittany on the Atlantic coast. Now, twenty years after Carolyn's first visit, we are working together. Through telling my story and Hamilton's, we may come to understand why that should be. My sense is that Hamilton and I each had an agreement with the Angelic realm long before we came into this incarnation. It would be our task to work with the stones of Carnac, to establish a connection with the ancient wisdom held there, then to present the information revealed to us to as many others as possible—people who might well be waiting to hear it. During the early stages of writing our first book, *Let The Standing Stones Speak*, I had moments of doubt, when I felt that some of this received information had been said before in different ways by the mystics of the past; surely the information was already out there, waiting for those interested enough to find it.

"Do we really have to do this?" I wondered.

Then I dreamed that night of being a runner in a relay race held in the darkness of night. At first, I was standing to one side, passed by hundreds of running torchbearers each with a raised arm bearing a flaming torch. But as one torchbearer stepped out of the race I was handed their torch, and so began my part in the relay. I understood that the torch of truth is a living flame that each one of us has the power to make burn more brightly. We simply have to keep the wisdom of the flame alive and run with it.

I do not separate Angels from stones; to me they are intertwined, stone being perhaps the most ancient life-form on Earth. I recently attended an exhibition of photographs of megaliths hung to publicize a book about the belief system of the Maori people of New Zealand. The exhibition had a surprising title—*Stones are our Ancestors*—a reference to Maori sacred places marked by standing stones at focal energy points.* According to the Maori, Archangels may also be our ancestors. This may sound strange, but science tells us that life on Earth was seeded from the stars, and mythology tells us that life originated with star-beings; thus, we are all stardust (or frozen light as it has been called). Our lives and personalities are patterned on archetypal qualities and our bodily systems regulated by planetary influences.

I see the Angelic world as guardian of the physical world. Of course, Angels may be present without the stones, but they apparently have found anchorage points around the prehistoric megaliths. One of the reasons the stones might have been placed where they are is that they are invariably situated on energy paths, the so-called ley lines (which we prefer to call solar lines.)

Writing *Let the Standing Stones Speak* gave us a greater understanding of our connection as humans to the unseen powerful forces at work in the Universe. That understanding is so needed today—to help people live in a more positive way, to feel connected to a greater plan, and to experience the infinite love of the Universe, which becomes apparent when we allow it into our hearts.

I had never heard of Carnac until some years ago when, during a healing session, my healer "saw" a field full of standing stones that she said were in France. She followed up by saying, "And that is where you have to go." At the time it did not resonate at all, and it was only later, when Hamilton and I were together, that I felt the importance of this vision.

Hamilton was interested in history and archaeology and was aware of Carnac. He suggested a trip there after we saw a picture on a small biscuit tin while visiting my cousin on Dartmoor in Devon—another place of many standing stones and circles. The picture showed the field of standing stones in the famous Carnac alignments. I was entranced. Soon afterward, we set off to find them. Only when we got there, did we realize how many neolithic sites remain in this part of Brittany: it has the largest concentration of standing stones in Europe.

While working on our book, we met many wonderful people in Brittany. After the book was published, many more contacted us to express their joy at the inspiration they received from it. Most of these people were also working to understand what are called Earth Mysteries, the energies around which the archaic wisdom schools were formed. The energies remain mysterious. They seem to imply that there is an even greater consciousness at work in the Universe than we know.

---

* *In Search of the Southern Serpent* by Hamish Miller & Barry Brailsford (Cornwall, UK: Penwith & Stone Print Press, 2006).

With its publication the book was completed, but apparently our work at Carnac was not. When Carolyn contacted us, and we three began to compare notes, we realized there was still more to do. Other experiences—both ours and Carolyn's, which were previously unrecorded—can now be told. And having made our first efforts on our own with invisible helpers, this time our writing is in happy cooperation with a fellow human! So here begins our journey...

Part One

1

Carolyn's Journal

I. Kercado

IN THE EARLY 1980s, I saw a picture of the passage mound at Kercado in a book about megalithic monuments in France. I immediately recognized it, but I had no idea why since I had never gone there, nor had I even been to that part of France. Not only was the mound familiar but, when I looked at the picture, I felt an odd sadness and an urge to go *back*. I also felt I had to invite a friend to go with me, a particular friend from Switzerland named Jiri whom I had not seen in a decade. Strange!

Jiri was a Czech Jew living and working as a chemist in Switzerland who, ten years before, had looked me up in California at the recommendation of his German girlfriend in Basel. I had met her earlier in the Galapagos Islands, in Ecuador, and we had become friends. For Jiri and I to have met at all in this lifetime meant that three people—a Czech, a German, and an American—had to each find themselves in a particular place in the world at a particular time and make a connection. But it had happened. From the first moment Jiri and I shook hands on a street corner in California, we recognized each other. It was clear why our mutual friend had wanted us to meet.

He was a fun-loving, bright guy, twelve years younger than me, who enjoyed many of the things I loved: hiking in all weathers, flying kites in the hills. We would go to the beach and wander until the sun set, or sit around the fireplace with my family, toasting marshmallows and sharing stories about our lives. He got along well with my husband; to my children he was like a grown-up playmate. It had been like saying goodbye to a sibling when we had parted.

Fire was a subject that seemed to come up often with Jiri. He told me two of his dreams: one of his house burning down and one about mine on fire. Once, while staying at our house, he spent the night feeding a fire in our fireplace, using up much of the wood in our woodpile. It was a bit weird, but I paid it little mind

The Kercado dolmen

because he was a bit of an odd duck to begin with. Part of what I liked so much about him was his unconventionality.

Not knowing what else to do, that spring, when the urge to travel to Brittany and to invite Jiri had become something of a compulsion, I consulted a woman in town who practiced psychic counseling and asked her for help in clarifying this unusual situation. It did not occur to me to mention any background about Jiri to her—only that I was thinking of taking a trip with this man from Switzerland whom I had not seen in a decade.

Right away, though, she said: "I see a fire—something awful!" She wrinkled her brow with distaste. "A burning, I think, like a witch burning. The last thing she sees is the man who betrayed her. A terrible death..."

I left the psychic's office feeling thoroughly shaken but believing none of it. I decided to drop this rather wild idea of going to France with someone I hadn't seen in years, for whom I wasn't even sure I had a current address. But two weeks later I was still thinking about Brittany, and some days later I found Jiri's telephone number and made the call. He answered right away. Mentioning nothing about fires, I said only that I was thinking of going to see the megaliths in Brittany and would he like to come.

"I would love to make a trip with you in old Europa!" he exclaimed, "but anywhere except *Bretagne*. I was there once, and it scared me. Let's go to Scotland."

"*Bretagne*," I said softly, certain by this time that Brittany was where I had to go. "I can't tell you why, but the stones at Carnac are calling me."

"And you wish to go with me?" he asked incredulously.

"I think so."

He was silent for several moments, then said; "I'll arrange it at work. I can take off a week."

And indeed, that June, late on the day of the full moon, we were together in Brittany, shouldering our backpacks and hiking up the hill behind the Carnac town dump, following a faint path in the grasses toward the site of the Kercado passage-mound I had seen in the book.

It was on private land not then officially open to the public, and the property owners—who lived in a small château on the other side of the woods—neither publicized the dolmen nor kept people out. If you could find the way on your own and respected the place, you were welcome, but the guidebooks barely mentioned that it existed and the roadways had no signs.

We made our way around the smelly dump and started climbing toward the modern water tower that, we were told, indicated the approximate location. At one point the trail forked and we stood there perplexed. We had no idea which path to take until Jiri noted a random scattering of sticks and a feather that seemed to point in one direction. We laughed about the appearance of "signs" but took that fork anyway. It led us right to the site.

In the lowering light the area around the covered mound was green and tranquil, a small clearing surrounded by pines and the modern water tower on the hillside. In its midst stood the dolmen covered in gorse and grass and its menhir, a standing stone of granite, on its crown. A small dark entryway opened, on one side, into the passage and chamber. Surrounding the mound was an incomplete circle of stones. Some were hidden in the trees and some exposed, one or two lying on the ground and others missing. The feeling of the place was sweet, with an undercurrent of sadness, similar to what I had sensed when I first saw the picture. I did not understand what I was feeling.

After putting down our backpacks and circling the mound in silence, we each found our way to separate stones, Jiri to one just opposite the entry, and me to the menhir on top. Without having said a word, we took our places facing one another as if we had planned it. Here is what I wrote in my journal about what came next:

> We sat facing each other for a long while, as the darkness deepened and the stars began to come out. It felt appropriate for us to be facing each other, as the stones themselves have faced each other these 5,000 years, and in the lowering light I felt something balancing within me. It was as if my stone was feminine and his masculine, and together they, and we, created a balance. I took a deep breath, and somewhere inside sensed a voice saying, *Good.*
>
> Eventually Jiri rose and came up the hill to sit beside me in the prickly gorse at the base of my stone. No words. Finally he sighed and said,
>
> "What I have always wished for is symmetry. I am partially deaf, and never feel like I am balanced."
>
> We spoke softly in French, even though English was the language we had used with each other in California. I told him about wondering if these were meant to be balancing stones. He nodded and rose to a stand, pulling me with him.
>
> We stood facing each other on either side of the stone. It was quite dark and the moon, full tonight, had not yet risen. Trying to read his eyes in the gloom confused me, because his face was not his face as I knew it, and his eyes didn't have the brilliance they had in daylight. I hardly recognized him.

We stared at each other for a long time but I couldn't find him. I was at this place with a stranger.

Now, yellow through the trees, the full moon began to appear. Slowly lighting her way through branches and sky, she seemed to be calling together a trio of women: the stone, the moon, and me. This unknown man by my side was excluded from our group.

Then I heard the word, *Dance!*

Something moved me away from the stone, and irresistibly I began to dance. I swung and circled and stamped, and knew the moon and stone were dancing along with me. They urged me to dance full out and hold nothing back. So I did. It was the weirdest experience I had ever had, but it felt absolutely right. Jiri leaned uncomfortably against the stone looking miserable. I had forgotten about him.

Well, too bad. He was free to dance if he wished, but if he didn't then that was his problem. I was amazed at how vehement my feelings were and had no idea where they came from. I boiled with anger and wanted to hurt him as he had hurt me... where had that come from?

It didn't matter. I flung out my arms and danced stronger, avoiding his eyes. He complained about feeling cold.

"So dance!" I taunted him derisively.

"I will!" he shouted, taking up the challenge and stamping around like an angry elephant. The moon rose higher, growing whiter and more beautiful, spreading light onto the top of the mound, which made me dance bigger, leaping and twirling. That made him furious and he pounded the ground with his feet.

"This is the way I danced when they burned you," he spat out.

What? Had I just heard what I thought I heard? I hadn't mentioned to him what I'd learned from the psychic, had I?

Keep dancing! The words came from I don't know where.

"No wonder they burned you if you danced like that!" Jiri was breathing hard as he kept up his stamping, and watching me closely.

Don't stop dancing, I heard.

My head was in fragments. What the hell was going on here?

I heard myself taunt him back: "What did you do when they burned me?" I could hardly believe I said that.

"I was excited," he told me, spitting out the words one by one. "I danced around the fire like mad!'

In my heart, I begged him not to say that, then I felt a jolt of power in my legs and took off like a whirling dervish. Whoever he was, I did not need him. The moon and the stone were my companions and I let the hurt flow off me like water.

Continuing to dance hard, I challenged him: "What would you do if they tried to burn me now?"

His reply was immediate and firm.

"I would protect you," he said, but spoiled it by adding with a laugh, "but nobody would burn you now."

Damn him!

"But if they did?" I demanded through clenched teeth. I wanted to kick him. "I would protect you, of course," said this stranger, coming closer and looking, in the moonlight, more like the Jiri I knew. In the end, he danced—not so much with me as alongside me.

Hold nothing back, I heard. Speak to him of what you know. Right now, or never again in this lifetime.

So I spoke to him of the fire and what I learned from the psychic, listening with astonishment to the words coming out of my mouth. He took me seriously, though, and responded with equal intensity and honesty. We talked to each other as if this story was all true and we were not pretending: a witch burning on this site, a love affair between an herbal healer and a local farmer, a frightened family. Neither of us believed in this kind of thing—Jiri is a scientist, after all—but there we were, recalling betrayal and violence from some time long before our own era.

And when we had each said to each other all that we could say, gentled by the ease with which we managed to say the words, the moon was almost gone from the top of the sky and we stumbled down the mound, spread out our sleeping bags, and fell into a dreamless sleep until morning.

In the stillness of the next morning, with birds out for their morning foraging, before we spoke even a greeting to one another we linked arms and very slowly danced together, barefoot on the grass alongside the dolmen.

II. Kerbachique and Kercado

OUR PLAN WAS to head out into the countryside surrounding the Gulf of Morbihan to search out other megalithic sites in the region, camping under the stars wherever we found ourselves each night. After we returned, in a week, we would explore Carnac—the alignments and the Tumulus St-Michel.

That first morning at Kercado we moved slowly, both quite shaken by what had transpired the night before. We crawled inside the chamber of the dolmen—one of the oldest known sites in Europe, according to our guidebook—and sat for a long time in the dark surrounded by slabs of granite reeking of the mold of ages. For thousands of winters, this dolmen had rested here on this hillside, witness to generations of people performing the rituals that marked the passages in their lives.

"Who were they, I wonder?" I mused. Jiri ran his hand along the rough face of the capstone above our heads, which alone must have weighed tens of tons.

"People like us, I imagine," he said, "who knew a science we no longer know. There is no way men could have moved all this rock by sheer strength alone."

After a while we crawled out backward and stood face to face, regarding each other with curiosity as if we were meeting for the first time. Who was this person who had arrived on my doorstep a decade ago, and what had brought us together again in this unlikely place? Could it really be that we had once, in another time, known each other *here* and had come back together to heal an ancient wound? It was outrageous enough to actually, possibly, be true. I smiled. Jiri smiled back, eyes crinkling at the corners of his broad Slavic face. Later, over a breakfast of toasted bread and hot chocolate, we said little but smiled a lot, amused to find ourselves again sitting by a fire in a beautiful place. He had insisted upon the fire.

"When you fall off a horse, you get on again," he remarked philosophically, with a logic uniquely his own. After the last crumb had been brushed away and our fire carefully doused we stood up, took each other's hands and hugged, agreeing to live only in the present for the next week, without referring again to the past.

"D'accord," we both murmured. "Agreed. We will be here now." He then turned to gather up our gear, rolling up the sleeping bags, while I packed up our meal. By noon we were ready to leave and, circumambulating the covered dolmen one last time, we made our way down the hill to where his car was parked, and took off toward the west.

On the road map, tiny stylized dolmens indicated megaliths and we followed them from one to the next. Driving along winding country roads, we would approach a village where a megalithic site had been indicated and, if we did not see it right away, ask directions. Half the people we stopped seemed not to know what we were asking for, but others were glad to engage with us, regarding us with great curiosity. They would point the way to this farmer's field, or that churchyard over there, or the outskirts of town, always wanting to know why we were interested.

"We are historians of the neolithic," Jiri would inform them with a straight face, chortling only after we had continued on. Most of the stones we found were unmarked and unattended: they had just always been there, several townsfolk told us. One grizzled farmer, when asked how old he thought the tall menhir in his barnyard was, observed, "Oh, very, very old. It was here when my grandfather was born."

When the stones were hidden in woods or a far field, we often located them by feeling for what we called *les energies*. We would close our eyes until we sensed a subtle buzz, then turn slowly in place until the buzz tugged us in one direction or another. For me, it came as an almost imperceptible pressure in my throat. For Jiri, it came as a throbbing in his temple, like the beginnings of a headache, he said. We tended to agree on the direction, though.

At the village of Kerbachique, the signal was strong enough to make us both feel slightly woozy. Jiri led the way through woods and across fields while I followed, the buzz growing stronger and more definite as we climbed a fence and went around a château until we found ourselves in a bucolic meadow of wildflowers where stood a pair of giant menhirs about 150 feet apart. The air all but vibrated with them.

On our hike across hill and dale we had felt fine, but coming into the energy fields of these two tall stones it was as if we had crashed into a wall. Jiri doubled over with a crushing migraine and I lost my balance, both of us scrambling out of range of the strong force and slumping to the ground beneath an oak tree, panting. Recovering in the shade, on our backs in the tall grass, we laughed at ourselves.

"Two great explorers from the city," he croaked. "Historians of the neolithic," I croaked back. "We shall not be vanquished by pieces of rock!" he vowed. We both giggled nervously.

We napped until we felt stronger after our impromptu initiation, and with great respect for the power of these stones, we retraced our steps back to them slowly, allowing ourselves to get used to the energies bit by bit. It took a while before it felt safe to be close to them. Once we could hold our own, we each chose a stone to stand against, facing each other and waiting to see what might happen.

What happened was, once again, a dance. Jiri's right arm lifted to the side and I did the same with my left. We took turns bending, lifting, twisting in slow gestures that the stones themselves seemed to be guiding, copying each other's movements to an unsung rhythm, *dum dada dum, dum dada dum*... The dance seemed

The Kerderff menhirs

to dance itself. My awareness opened to hot sun and the roughness of warm granite against my back, to birdsong in the air, the ripe green sweetness of the wildflower meadow. *Dum dada dum, dada dum...* A melody rode the repeated rhythm I was hearing in my mind's ear, a curling song imposed upon a ground bass.

When I sang it out loud, Jiri repeated it back to me. Then I sang it back to him and he returned it, adding his own improvisation. Then me, changing it again. Then him, embellishing my phrase before returning it to me. The song sang itself back and forth between us, call and response, sometimes fast, sometimes slow, sometimes loud, sometimes soft as a whisper, but always effortless, beautiful.

By the time we stopped, my chest felt too small to hold my heart. I was in a state of utter happiness and had no idea how much time had gone by. The sun was lowering, the stones casting long shadows in the field, the air was fragrant and between us was the sweet ease of shared delight. Staring at each other, we knew we had experienced something brand new. Just as the night before, we had no idea what had just happened nor how, but we knew that being here together at this particular moment in our lives was exactly right.

III. St-Guyomard

IN THE REGION surrounding the town of St-Guyomard are several megalithic sites. We explored most of them: huge menhirs of quartz that made us dizzy; dolmens in various states of collapse; a Christian chapel built next to a *fontaine,* or spring, whose waters, the locals said, had cured people of rheumatism since time immemorial.

At each place we approached the stones respectfully and waited to feel for what might be there. At certain stones we felt calmed, at others energized. Sites that had been destroyed mostly felt sad to us—a little sour. Sites that felt welcoming encouraged us to draw nearer. At one dolmen in a wood, Jiri stretched out on top of a fallen stone and fell into a sudden, irresistible sleep. When he awoke, he had no idea where he was.

"What!" he spluttered fuzzily. "Was I asleep?"

"Out like a light," I said.

"Who woke me up?" he demanded in confusion.

It took several minutes, and much muttering, before he was completely awake. We left that place quickly without looking back.

On the afternoon of the summer solstice, we followed the dolmen logos on the map to the small village of Moustoir-Ac, near St-Guyomard, hoping to find the perfect megalithic site to spend the night. We wanted it to be beautiful, feel welcoming, and be remote enough for us to camp there privately. A smallish dolmen by the side of the road with a rounded capstone had not fit the bill, so we spread the map out on the ground to search for the next likely place. My throat immediately swelled with pressure and I felt a tug coming from the field on the other side of the road, which was tall with ripening rapeseed. Beyond the field rose a wooded hill. Jiri grew very still.

"Feel it?" he asked softly.

I nodded. "Let's go."

We grabbed our backpacks, climbed the fence, and made our way through the rustling grain to where the woods started at the base of the hill.

Through the dense trees we blazed a trail, stopping periodically to feel for the buzz, sometimes with Jiri leading the way and sometimes me. About halfway up the hill, in what was barely a clearing, we found it—a huge dolmen built into an

A hidden dolmen

outcrop of rounded boulders, its capstone protruding beyond the last of the supporting rocks. It looked as if it had not been visited in decades. Breathless, we dropped our backpacks and bent over to peer inside.

Indomitable, Jiri crawled right in. I followed and was immediately swallowed by the dark. The chamber went deep into the hillside, into unbroken darkness. Jiri was right in front of me, but I couldn't see him. I swiveled around to be reassured by the light at the opening, but it did not penetrate more than about two feet into the chamber. I stayed close to him, frightened by this place.

Moments later we reemerged, crawling backward toward the entrance, both of us subdued and in need of solitude. Saying few words, Jiri took off to explore, leaving me leaning against a supporting boulder and staring contemplatively into the forest. By the time he reappeared, I had unpacked for our evening meal and was ready to do some exploring myself.

"There's a small pond back there," he said, pointing. "Not too far. Follow the deer trail."

I heard it before I saw it, the sounds of birds whirring and dipping reaching me on the breeze. The edges of the pond were marshy and lined with reeds, and the surface reflected the steep-angled sun. For a long time I perched on a pondside rock, watching the quick movements of birds.

I wondered again who had once lived here and why they had constructed all these massive stoneworks. For such an enormous task—hundreds of tons of rock moved all over the landscape—people had to have a very good reason. Now, though, the stones lay disused and forgotten. Why did I have such a strong sense that we were being asked to remember, Jiri and me? What had those long-ago builders known that humans had since forgotten? How could we find out?

When I arrived back at the dolmen, daylight was fading and Jiri was gone. I tried not to panic, but my heart pounded in fear. I called out to him, but the only response I got was a faint echo of my own voice. Our gear had been neatly unpacked and our sleeping bags laid out side by side in the opening to the chamber. He couldn't have gone far. It grew darker and darker with the coming of night, and by the time he returned I was shaking.

"Where were you?" he scolded, as he emerged from the woods.

"Right here," I replied, weak with relief.

"But I *was* here!" he insisted.

"Well, I stayed for a while at the pond, but not that long," I protested. "And I've been here for about an hour since then."

He claimed that when I didn't return, he took the deer trail to the pond to find me, but I wasn't there, and when he came back I wasn't here, and he certainly couldn't have missed me on the trail. "I went back twice!" he cried, almost in tears. We were both quaking, scared by this place that had the power to make us invisible to each other, but it was too late to pack up and leave. There was nothing for it but to stay and brave it out.

"Maybe we're in a different dimension here," he teased later, after we'd gotten a fire blazing merrily and had hot soup from a package warming our bellies. "Maybe that's why it's not on the map. Maybe we've been abducted by fairies and we'll never see home again."

"Well, we asked for mysterious. Maybe we should watch out what we ask for," I retorted.

But it was all bravado. Actually, we were both scared out of our wits.

We crept into our sleeping bags, a flashlight by our heads just in case, and fell into a deep sleep until I was jolted awake by a bright light shining in my face. I grabbed for the flashlight and sat up, my heart pounding in my throat. But the light was the moon shining through the trees, right into the opening of the chamber. It lit us up like a spotlight. I shook him awake to see it, but after mumbling something in Czech, Jiri drifted off again.

I stayed awake, though, to watch the moon silver us with its light as it slipped gradually away from center, moving across me, then Jiri. For a few moments he was radiant with cool moonlight, fast asleep. Smiling, I blessed this person who had found me from across the world, and perhaps also across time, and kissed his brow. Jiri slept on.

Later, I bolted awake again. The moon was no longer lighting the dolmen, but something was in the chamber with us. Dry leaves crackled, and I felt it creeping closer and closer. Jiri woke up this time and grabbed for the flashlight, bravely aiming it in the direction of the intruder. I was certain we were about to see a sight no human has ever lived to describe, when into the beam of our light came... a toad! It stopped, blinking, then leapfrogged away deeper into the chamber. Rustle, rustle. We collapsed onto our backs laughing, and as dawn was already graying the sky we gave up the idea of sleeping and just lay there talking.

"Once," he mused, "people must have come here to celebrate on the solstices. Can you picture them coming up the hill in the dark?"

"Everyone in the village," I continued, "kids and old people. What do you suppose went on inside the chamber?"

"I'd guess it was some kind of initiation about learning how to go from visibility to invisibility," he conjectured. "Something about dimensions, I don't know." We both shivered and dozed off again in the quiet of that quietest hour before dawn.

The sun had yet to penetrate the gloom, but soon we were awakened by birds twittering in the trees all around us. Jiri yawned. We both lay back, thinking our own thoughts until the sun, rising above the trees, shone hot in our faces. We clambered out of the dolmen and stretched luxuriously. By daylight, the site was innocent of mysterious presences.

We gathered together the cooking gear, rolled up our sleeping bags, helped each other hoist our packs onto our backs, and started back down the hill. Within a few yards, we could no longer see the dolmen. I was tempted to run back and make sure it was still there, but Jiri wouldn't let me.

"Maybe it's just our eyes are bad," he declared. But he took out his camera anyhow and, leaning against a tree to steady his hands, took a picture of the place where we had last seen the dolmen—a leafy tangle of woods.

"So we know we're not crazy," he explained with his whimsical grin.

IV. Le Golfe du Morbihan

AFTER OUR SCARY NIGHT at the dolmen, we decided to take a break from exploring megaliths and drove toward the sea. Late in the day, we found ourselves in a fishing village and checked into a small *pension* by the water for a night on the town: baths, laundry, and dinner in a restaurant. Strolling down to a sandy cove by the pier, we stood watching the sun set over the sea, talking little, taking in the salt softness of the air and feeling rather pleased with ourselves. The wavelets lapped at our toes in their uneven rhythm, and my feet followed their in-and-out motion in a small, stepping dance. Jiri began to hum, then danced his own two-step, while I added my voice quietly to his. Our duet ebbed and flowed at the tideline.

The song we sang was as natural as breathing, and our melodies, spinning and spilling around each other, were in perfect harmony. We relaxed into our impromptu creation as if we had been singing like this all our lives. The song, new in each moment and hauntingly beautiful, accompanied the sun as it moved closer to the water, growing orange, then red, the clouds glowing green, then pink above us, the dusk deepening gradually and then quickly into darkness, until only a faint bar of light still hovered above the sea.

Our duet was an oratorio, an opera. We were brilliant, the two of us, and sang a song brand new and as old as the world. We had been singing it since the beginning of time, and our voices knew the notes perfectly. We caught each other's eye and incorporated into the song a lovely, wild giggle.

Eventually, though, it ended on a pure unison note that we held until all breath ran out. For a while, we did not move but stayed right there at the edge of the water, hands clasped and gazing out at the night-time sea.

"Supper?" Jiri finally suggested softly. We turned and walked up the beach toward the restaurant, and there feasted on celery root salad, spicy bouillabaisse, Camembert cheese— and each other.

Some entrancement had overtaken us, and we were both bamboozled. We were drunk, breathless—and it wasn't the wine. Maybe the stones had bewitched us. Maybe we thought we were back in that other time. We were playing with fire, and we both knew it. But none of that mattered because whatever was going on, there was no mistaking the glory and gladness at being together in the world, the swelling of the heart, the thrill at every little thing that is the rapture of falling in love.

Until that evening, we had been content to sleep in separate sleeping bags, change our clothes in full view of each other, and never consider each other as potential lovers. I was married with children; he was twelve years my junior. We were just taking an unusual kind of vacation, that's all. Granted, our relationship was not an ordinary one, but we were two contemporary people living in the modern world. Much stranger things have happened. Right?

So, in our happily tipsy state, we made our way upstairs to our shared room, not quite sure what would happen but feeling open to whatever did, just like in our improvised song.

Of course, we fell right into each other's arms. A moment later, however, I had the strong impression that we were not alone in our room. Jiri must have felt it, too, because we disentangled and gave each other a puzzled look.

Are you absolutely sure? I heard.

I had no idea where this came from, but the warning was clear to both of us. We laughed uneasily and tried to ignore it, embracing again, but there was still the spooky sensation of a presence in the room with us. Twice more we tried to ignore the warning but it was all in vain, and finally we gave up, laughing instead.

"This is not the right moment," Jiri declared with mock solemnity, and after bestowing upon each other a chaste kiss, we climbed into separate beds and fell into a deep sleep until the morning.

V. The Isle of Gavrinis

WE RETURNED TO CARNAC by way of the coast, exploring the extensive inlets of the Gulf of Morbihan, and took a tourist boat from Larmor-Baden to the tiny isle of Gavrinis and its grand, restored passage mound, much larger than Kercado and at least as ancient. Approaching by boat was thrilling. On the way, we passed another island, somewhat tilted, with a half-submerged circle of stones slipping beneath the waves. The tour guide explained that this watery channel was once dry land, and that the stone circle we saw was actually intertwined with another one concealed beneath the waves.

"Tonight, we'll come and dive with flashlights," whispered the irrepressible Jiri.
"Yes," I whispered back.

On the carefully fenced, guarded, and reconstructed Gavrinis, we were not permitted to leave the confines of the group.

"We will escape when they are loading the boat and camp here tonight," whispered Jiri.

"Of course," I whispered back, stifling a grin. Later, though, when we tried to evade the tour guide, we were apprehended and herded back onto the boat for the return trip.

We were the last ones to enter the mound, remaining outside to feel for the energies in the surrounding area. But no matter where we stood, we felt nothing.

Engraving on stone

"They've taken away the wildness," Jiri complained, slapping a hand on the modern concrete construction covering the mound. The tour guide came back to make sure we went in with the others, clearly keeping an eye on the two bad kids in his class, and we followed the last people into the long passageway. Once inside, however, we were stopped by a sight that knocked the breath out of us.

The interior walls were covered with lines of swooping, curving, spiraling designs, whorl after whorl of intersecting arcs and concentric circles. All around us, they whirled in intricate, dizzying patterns that seemed to be in motion. Off balance, I leaned against the wall of the narrow passageway where, through my light shirt, I could feel the close spacing of the curving lines that once long ago had been incised into this rock and hidden from the light of day.

Who would have performed this huge task, and how? Who were they doing it for, and why? *Why?* How come the extraordinary people who had once lived right here were completely unknown to us now? How come we had lost whatever it was they had understood? I had no idea but hoped the stones would give me my clue sometime in the next two weeks.

VI. Return to Carnac

DRIVING BACK TO CARNAC and our last two days together, Jiri and I postponed the return to "real life" with its proprieties, schedules, and our inevitable leave-taking. We took long walks on the shore and stopped at cafés in every town we passed. We talked to children, to fishermen, to shopkeepers. We hung out on piers, looking at the yachts and fishing boats. We reminisced about our trip and told each other stories we had not told before.

This parting, we both knew, would be for good. The fact that we had met up in this life at all was something of a miracle; however, it had happened, and we had apparently accomplished what we were supposed to. The stones may have helped us in ways we could not fathom but, imagined or real, we had somehow found each other in the world to heal and regain a kinship that had once been lost.

Even if we were making the whole thing up, both our lives had been transformed by our week together. In fact, the story was so unlikely that for the next twenty years I would speak of it to almost nobody. At the time, however, it was just what was happening and, neither of us being quite ready to let go, we were going to live our last two days together to the hilt. The plan was to find me a place to stay in Carnac for the next fourteen days, to explore the Carnac area together, and spend our last night camping somewhere at the alignments.

The Briard family, whose home was within walking distance of the sea at Kerfraval, was pleased to get a paying guest who would stay two full weeks; they offered to lend me a bicycle, as well. The family lived within the shadow of the Kercado hill—which they had never visited, they told us—and offered me a front room with a view of the water, promising it would be ready when I came back two days later.

Jiri and I made straight for the alignments. They were about a mile away, a swath of standing stones, twelve rows across, running through the countryside for three miles just inland from the coast. The approximately three thousand stones currently in existence had once been more like ten thousand stones, we were told. The lines of stones, at that time unfenced, were interspersed with small hamlets, farms, and pastures, where cows and horses grazed. Few visitors disturbed the pastoral peace of the place.

We stood where the alignments began, at Le Ménec. From here, we could see row upon row of stones marching in procession across the flat countryside, stretching all the way to the horizon. We could not see where they ended. Jiri took my hand and we walked solemnly into their company, surrounded on every side by carefully placed stones that had no known history, no story to go along with them, only conjecture. They had already been ancient in the time of Christ; even then, their provenance must have been a mystery.

They were beautiful. Each stone was a different shape. Each row, twelve across, started with great, looming menhirs that grew smaller and smaller as the row progressed, until that section ended with a stone circle. A bit farther on, the next section of stone rows began, again with enormous menhirs that gradually progressed into smaller ones. We walked down the rows as if in a trance.

In Paris, not to mention California, friends claimed to know nothing of the megaliths in Carnac. The south coast of Brittany was known for its beaches, its healing baths, and its sailing. Parisians, I was told, preferred to visit the north coast; the south coast was mostly a holiday place for Dutch and German families who came for the beaches.

On this day, in fact, even though it was a beautiful summer afternoon, we pretty much had the stones to ourselves as we wandered down and across the rows. Their sheer volume was overwhelming, but when we stopped and felt for the energies, neither of us could feel much of a buzz. What we had experienced out in the countryside all week had been considerably more pronounced and easier to read.

"They must come to life at night," Jiri concluded, regarding the bulk of shaped granite beside him. Perhaps the magic and intimacy of the individual, out-of-the-way stones we had found in the villages was simply not here in all this immensity, or perhaps we were both tired. We decided to leave the alignments and go to the beach. "We shall come back later," said my friend.

The Kermario rows

The tides at Carnac go way out, leaving broad, rippled mudflats and exposing lovely sand islands easily reachable by causeways of solid ground. A few people could be seen lounging in the dunes on one of these islands, so we took off our boots and went out to join them. Mud squished coolly between our toes and the sun dappled the faraway water with light, as we made our way across the wet sand to the island. On a dune hidden from the mainland shore by bunches of seagrass, we stretched out to sunbathe in preparation for our night awake at the stones, and fell fast asleep.

It was very still when we awoke. The other sunbathers on the island had gone. The sun was slanting shadows of wind-blown grasses on the sand, and the sound of lapping water lulled our senses. We dozed some more—then sat up, bolt awake. The tide had come in. We were stranded!

My first reaction was fear. Then Jiri roared with laughter, and I had to also.

"I love us!" he snorted. "We are so stupid together that we have the best time! I shall lead us out of the wilderness like a desert father," he promised, "but first, I must test the waters to see if they are over our heads."

It took us a while, but we eventually made it back, wading in water up to our chests, our backpacks perched lopsided on our heads and our pants rolled up to our thighs. A few people on the shore watched our progress wondering, no doubt, about these probably drunk tourists, and we received much applause and laughter when we made it to shore. The owner of a nearby café wanted to hear our story, which we outdid each other in making up. Then, after a wonderful supper of sausages and dark beer, we retrieved the car, changed into dry clothes, and shouldered our sleeping bags, backpacks, and a few pieces of driftwood for a night at the alignments.

We chose a section of stones in a place called Kermario, about halfway through the alignments. Few people made it this far, so the ground between the menhirs was untrampled and covered in tall ferns and gorse bushes. The stones stood like silent sentinels, as they had done for millennia, and I felt a sense of welcome there. Jiri claimed to feel it, too.

"It's like they are relieved to know we have come," he remarked.

"How may we be of service?" he announced loudly, speaking directly to the stones. We sat very still listening for an answer, and even though we were more or less play-acting, an answer seemed to come.

Listen.

I heard it; Jiri heard it. Both of us, somewhat spooked by the immediate response, got busy building a firepit out of small rocks and pebbles and searched around for kindling. Once we had a fire going, Jiri spoke again. "We are listening," he said purposefully.

Le Ménec alignments

Awaken yourselves, awaken us.

I received this not as words in any language but as a complex set of feelings and images that showed me how my own awakening into a mindful state of clear intention could spark the intelligence residing in these standing stones. The intelligence was sluggish now, I intuited, because humans had not evoked it for too long a time, and it was urgent that it be evoked now. This, and much more, was somehow implicit in the quick impressions that came through to both of us.

As we watched the flames of our fire take hold, we quietly checked out with each other the sense of the information we had each received, and how it had appeared to us. Jiri saw pictures, schema—for me it was more a felt "knowing," deeper than thought; but our understandings of what came through matched perfectly and augmented each other's impressions. The more we talked about what we had received, the more richly our comprehension was fleshed out. We understood that the stones needed humans to be activated, and that they had not been properly attended to for centuries. We realized that our coming was a gift both to them and to ourselves, and that by doing the work of raising our own awareness, we would be doing the work of reactivating their work of bringing earth, life, and spirit into balance.

Jiri placed a piece of driftwood onto the burning kindling. We watched it spit and crackle, then burn brightly, sending light shadows onto the surrounding stones. The last hues of sunset were fading over the western horizon. We sat still, watching the dusk flare, then deepen in the evening sky.

"Okay, we hear you," I whispered, my breath unsteady. "Tell us what we can do right now." We still were not sure quite how seriously to take ourselves, but a moment later we received the same, unequivocal response.

Sing. For a while we just sat there staring into the fire.

"I heard *Sing*," murmured Jiri.

"*Sing*," I affirmed, surprised and yet not surprised at all that we had heard the same thing. So we sang. The song started out softly, more like sighs than like notes. Breath by breath, we attuned with each other until we could feel the resonance in our chests. The song seemed to sing itself, without us. While it spun itself out, my mind registered instructions, one by one, of how to prepare myself for my solitary two weeks in this region.

First came an insight, distilled into something like words, to choose three separate sites that I would visit each day—one early, one midday, and one late in the day. Each day I was to alternate locations for the different times of day. Kercado was, of course, to be one of these sites, and I was to pay especial attention to the menhir atop the mound.

Slow way down.
Get very still.
Listen closely.
Pay meticulous attention to what you feel at every moment.
Inside, feel. Outside, feel.
Keep a journal of everything you experience.

It could not have been clearer. Jiri reached across the embers of our fire and took my hands, tears in his eyes. There was nothing more to say; spirals of smoke curled between us, and we had each heard what was ours to hear. Jiri had his instructions; I had mine. They resonated in the air between us. We were not to speak of them to each other or to anybody, so as to maintain clear concentration. The instructions rang true, and I simply trusted them. The more unlikely this adventure became, the more I felt I was in the right place at the right time.

We were almost ready… almost. Right now we were still here together, having taken a strange road together that had brought us to a country of love. Sleep was out of the question, and we fed the fire with dried gorse, sitting close together against a tilted stone, holding hands and talking softly. We were amazed by all we had been through in this one week and were not quite ready to have it end. But it was almost time. Almost.

It was the darkest hour before first light when we slid down into our sleeping bags on the dewy ground, our heads close together against the base of the stone. We slept away our last few hours together and awoke with the dawn.

VII. Kerfraval

DOWN ON THE COAST ROAD I waved until Jiri's car went round a bend and out of sight. I stood in the light rain, staring at the space where he last had been. Now it was filled only with gray mist, sea, and an occasional seagull. No Jiri.

The sudden solitude pressed upon me like a weight and I turned slowly and walked back up the hill, past the modern stone houses in this suburb of Carnac, to my little room at the Briard's. I heard the sounds of the family downstairs: Papa, Maman, a teenaged daughter, and a boy about age six, but they did not come out. I entered and went quietly up the stairs, glad to be alone. I needed solitude right now.

For the rest of the day, I arranged my few things and lay on my bed musing and dozing, getting accustomed to the quiet as I had been instructed to do. Gazing out the window at mist and rain and the horse pasture across the way, I pictured Jiri crossing borders in his car, traveling farther and farther away from Brittany—and me—with each turn of the wheels.

The song you sing now will be your own song.

Already, the felt impression of teachings emerging into my consciousness was becoming more recognizable. The sensory images translated into words and phrases almost simultaneously now. When I understood their meaning, I responded with silent assent; I could feel a sweet settling in my body when I was heard, in turn. This was not then, nor is it now, an easy thing to describe. The only living person who might know what I was talking about was Jiri, who was elsewhere now, and the only people I knew in Carnac were the Briards. From now on, I would have nobody with whom I could talk—except the stones, of course.

Hunger finally drove me out. I rolled out of bed and walked slowly down the hill to the waterside café where we had eaten sausages the night before. Was it really only last night? I carried my guidebook and a brand new notebook that would become my journal for the next two weeks. Over a bowl of steaming onion soup, I decided on my three sites: Kercado; the Le Ménec alignments, visiting a different stone each day; and Tumulus St-Michel, a massive man-made hill of earth and rock that had been created for who knew what reason, long before the era of metal tools.

A small Christian chapel is now perched on top of Tumulus St-Michel but, according to the guidebook, the tumulus itself was built around a huge dolmen and was honeycombed with niches and chambers. My plan was to bike there in the morning and start my two-week retreat inside it. Toward noon I would go into the town, explore the outdoor market, and buy a picnic lunch to bring to Le Ménec for my afternoon stint. In the late afternoon, I would find my way back to Kercado.

In my guidebook I read the following description of Tumulus St-Michel:

> The series of small graves in the Tumulus go back beyond 4000 BC, and the mound itself may be much earlier... Archaeological findings have revealed a series of small dolmen-like chambers and cists, some holding human remains and grave goods, others containing animal bones. The idea that these little tombs could be the main reason for building this tremendous mound seems totally unconvincing. *

Walking back to the Briards' house, I imagined men laboring to construct such a mound. Where might they and their families have lived, and how did they sustain themselves? Perhaps I was walking on one of their fields, their houses. Who were these people?

That night I dreamed of home, and upon waking I felt homesick. Was I sure I was up to the task of taking on this odd assignment? No, but the best I could do was to try. I awoke to an overcast, but dry and windy day, and the croupy coughing of the little boy downstairs.

"Has he had this for a while?" I asked his mother, stopping in the kitchen on my way out.

"It's two months already," she complained. "He just won't stop coughing."

I watched him as he played with his toy airplane, coughing intermittently between making little-boy vroom-vroom noises. Dropping my backpack on the kitchen floor, I played with him, making vroom-vrooms of my own, to the astonishment of his mother. We caromed around the kitchen together, both of us being noisy airplanes.

In my mind's ear I could detect his healthy "note." I sang it back to him while we both ran around the kitchen like maniacs, until he and I dropped into a giggling heap on the floor. I tickled him while still singing his tone right into his belly.

Then I felt something shift in his body and, giving him a hug, I gathered up my

---

* *A Guide to the Megaliths of Europe* by Alastair Service and Jean Bradbery (Chicago: Academy Chicago Publishers, 1983).

backpack to leave while he wrapped himself around my knees to keep me there. The next day Madame Briard reported that, after screaming his head off all day, he had discharged large amounts of green mucous and now his cough was gone. What had I done?

I did not know, of course, although I was gratified that it had worked with little Pierre. I suspected help from the stones. Afterward, I was not so sure it had been such a good idea because his mother announced to the neighbors that an American healer was at their house for the next two weeks, had cured Pierre of his awful cough, and might be available should anyone else need healing.

2

Natasha

The angels keep their ancient places;
Turn but a stone and start a wing!
'Tis ye, 'tis your estrangéd faces,
That miss the many-splendoured thing.
—FRANCIS THOMPSON, In No Strange Land

Kerzerho and le Manio

SOON AFTER ARRIVING AT CARNAC, Hamilton and I made our first visit to the Kerzerho stone rows that can be seen beside the road near Erdeven. Looking out the car windows from the small parking area, we were surrounded by a thicket of huge standing stones and immediately felt we were among friends at a family reunion. They seemed to greet us warmly as we walked among them. These megaliths, some of them enormous, are not fenced in but look like a natural part of the Brittany countryside. They led us on to discover other stones hidden among the undergrowth in the woods and the fields.

That same afternoon, after our friendly welcome at Kerzerho, we made our way to the main alignments of Le Ménec, which were then also unfenced. It was there, standing beside the great stone called Le Géant, that I heard a loud voice in my head, saying, *This is a library, and you can read it.* Although the information was not altogether surprising, the strong voice was entirely unheralded.

The next day we familiarized ourselves with the whole extensive layout at the Carnac Museum of Prehistory, where the alignments are set out as a scale model that makes the stones look like rows of tiny teeth. Many of the original stones have been destroyed and others removed for building purposes. The church in Carnac incorporates stones taken from the alignments when it was rebuilt in 1639.

We thought about the stones being a kind of library, a store of information. If that were so, how should we begin to read it? We felt drawn to Le Géant du Manio, a large single menhir set in the woods away from the main alignments and

The Kerzerho rows

visited years before by Carolyn. It wasn't easy to locate. Rain was starting to fall and part of the muddy track was impassable, but eventually we found it in a clearing, a tall elegant presence leaning toward us, as though expecting our visit. Seated alongside the menhir as it looked down on us with benevolence, we felt humbled. It had assumed the bearing of a teacher, and I made notes of the information I began to receive.

Welcome, friends. You are very welcome and have been expected.

Among the alignments of this region you will find that certain stones hold information. They contain messages for the human race. It is your task to record them.

They are programmed into stone, and it is your enjoyable assignment, your prearranged destiny, to reveal them and pass them on to other people who are waiting to hear them.

The information is to help the human race in the present hour of need and give some guidance for the times of great confusion that are to follow.

These messages can only be received when there is silence in your heart and mind, when you are conscious only of being, not of doing, for it is then you are receptive to higher dimensions.

The source of this wisdom is all around you, but since most people have lost the ability to listen, it is preserved in this way, waiting to be heard by those who possess the quality of inner quietness.

After about an hour the rain became heavier, and when a group of people clad in raincoats arrived to pay a visit to our new friend, we gathered ourselves up, and with a rather damp notebook in hand, quietly took our leave.

Back at our hotel and too early for dinner, we relaxed in an anteroom with large gilded mirrors and elaborate old furniture. When I looked at my notes in this very different environment, I could hardly believe what I had written.

The stones at Carnac hold a message for the human race. It is your task to record this message.

Could it really be true that these ancient megaliths have a message for us, maybe also for the benefit of other people? Was it up to Hamilton and me to find and record it? At that time, writing a book had not crossed our minds nor how we were to share whatever messages we would receive. Somewhat stunned by the whole idea, we still managed to enjoy a good dinner while considering it all.

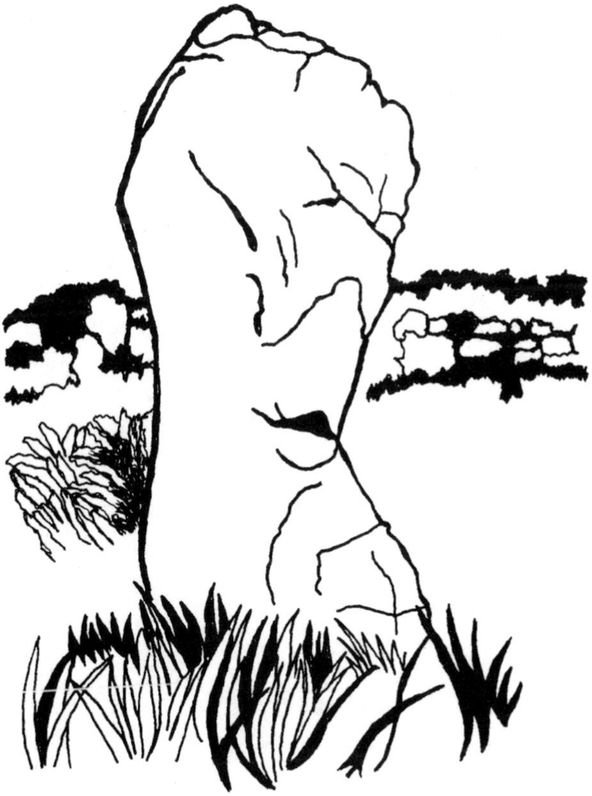

Le Géant du Ménec

The following day we felt drawn back to the Ménec alignments. We began selecting the most likely stones to hold more information for us and spent the next few days writing up notes and taking photographs for identification later on. As we were rather rushed for time, our approach at that point became too academic and we failed to honor the instruction from Le Géant, to quietly "be" rather than rush around "doing." Had we listened, we might have saved ourselves from a good deal of stress.

Later, back in England, after months spent working on the information received at these randomly chosen stones, I became very downhearted. It was not at all the uplifting guidance we had anticipated. We could not imagine anyone benefiting from this list of admonishments about the failures of the human race and our lack of care for the planet and each other. While it was all true enough, it could hardly be the message we were supposed to be seeking.

We decided to consult White Bull, the spirit of an American Indian whose philosophical teachings were at that time channeled through a friend of ours in London. In his usual warm and friendly fashion, he suggested to us that in an earlier incarnation, thousands of years ago, we had been involved in the placing of the stones at Carnac and had taken part in the original intention of setting out the alignments. This resonated deeply for us, as the powerful feelings of love emanating from the stones struck us not as human love but more like an aspiration for human love: love of the Earth itself and the Angelic realm combined.

But, he said, although the stones were expecting us and information was there for us to find, we had to show that we were able to distinguish a false message from a true one. We were being tested, and our task was to learn how to listen. We were to return to the alignments and make ourselves known to the stones, state our intention, and ask for their permission and cooperation. If it were sensed that we had acquired the necessary qualifications, we would be led to the particular stones we sought.

So we went back with a more respectful attitude, and this time there seemed to be a great chattering going on between the stone rows. Our intentions were apparently recognized because, with careful dowsing, again making use of the scale model, we were able to identify certain megaliths that were important for us. There were, it transpired, just five that we needed, and we went to each in turn—not without some problems of access—until their messages were, over time, revealed and could be committed to paper. It was clear then that we had found that the stones were transmitting a true and constructive message, not simply for us but one that needed to be shared with others.

Invisible Realms and the Elves

SOME TIME BEFORE my first visit to the megaliths of Carnac, I attended a series of healing workshops in which many of our sessions were focused on the invisible dimensions of life, the realms of Spirit. I received some wonderful insights, which gave me a deeper understanding of the visible world in which we live.

Gathered in a well-cared-for garden in the English countryside, surrounded by trees and flowers, the workshop leaders showed us how to calibrate our personal vibrations with those of the spirits of Nature, which, as we learned, coexist around all life-forms—animal, vegetable, and mineral: the American redwood tree to the alpine flower, the wren to the albatross, the smallest pebbles to the tallest mountain ranges.

For me, that was a time of training in attunement, where I was taught to be quiet enough to hear the voices of the natural world and to perceive with my inner eye things that normally go unseen. Most of us are closed to such phenomena, seeing only what lies on the surface and rarely perceiving the deeper rhythms of Nature. Thus, we miss their relevance, something once integral to our distant ancestors' lives.

One day, about twenty-five of us were seated in a circle. Glass sliding doors made the greenery of the beautiful garden outside seem like part of the room. Through them, we could see a huge willow tree swaying gently in the breeze, as though it wanted to be with us. Aware that healers and shamans of old could tune in to the spirit of a plant in order to ascertain its healing properties, we decided to invite the willow to join the group. Medicine has, of course, already made use of one variety of willow, *Salix alba,* as a main constituent of aspirin because of its pain-relieving properties, although now the effect is produced synthetically.

With our intention focused upon the willow tree, we silently called upon it to indicate its purpose to us. Our request, a quiet inner plea, quite suddenly and dramatically led to a tremendous shift in energy in the group, as everyone clearly sensed an animated force in the centre of the circle. Each of us perceived it in our own way; to me it appeared as a tall, very graceful being. As it began to send us information, we were individually shown the diverse healing properties in various parts of the tree—in the bark, the leaves, and so on—and could feel their healing power within our own bodies.

It was a profound encounter, experienced by people from different walks in life who were all interested in healing; hairdressers, an art teacher, therapists, nurses, even a blacksmith. But as we continued working with other Nature spirits, it gradually became evident to us that something was amiss.

Each species of plant may be regarded as the physical manifestation of a set of etheric vibrations. Beings who, for the sake of convenience, we call Nature spirits hold the blueprint for each plant. They keep it healthy according to its various functions, which might be for attracting pollinating insects such as bees or developing healing properties for specific ailments in humans and animals. For the plant to survive it requires appropriate sustenance, good soil conditions, sunlight, and access to clean air and water. For a Nature spirit to provide etheric sustenance, it must itself receive nourishment from a higher vibration. As we know, but were told again by the Nature spirits, humankind is increasingly polluting the atmosphere, while agriculture worldwide continues to replace many of the natural qualities and micro-organisms in the soil with synthetic fertilizers, robbing it of its life force. The extensive use of chemical substances not only upsets the ecological balance but also poisons our water supply. In fact, much of the grain now grown to feed the world population is infertile and cannot seed the next year's crop; in effect, it produces dead food.

What I did not know was that the spirits of Nature can hardly survive in an environment that lacks the life force, that mysterious, all-pervasive energy on which they and all living things are dependent. When a plant species becomes sick or dies, Nature spirits do also, along with the blueprint of the species. Having no individual souls, they return to their origin and merge with the energy field that we might call the "greater soul."

Nature spirits and other entities of the unseen realms are often called "the elementals." Elementals are beings composed of the four primary elements of living matter, long regarded as Earth, Air, Fire, and Water. Now science recognizes the four basic elements needed for physical life as carbon, oxygen, nitrogen, and hydrogen in various combinations. The traditional belief was that the many varieties of elementals, not having a physical structure, were less complex than humans and animals and were composed mainly of a single element.

Spirits of place—water, trees, rocks, and mountains—have long been fundamental to the animistic belief systems of indigenous peoples, still in existence in remote parts of the world. In classical Greek culture they were called nymphs, the female spirits of Nature, and dryads, the spirits of woods and trees. Still recognized today in the Indian pantheon and among Indonesian peoples, they survive in the faery tradition of northern European folklore. Many megalithic site names perpetuate these beliefs, as at the great dolmen of La Roche aux Fées in France. Tolkien made much play with them in his book series *The Lord of the Rings*, as did Shakespeare with *A Midsummer's Night's Dream.*

When I first encountered Nature spirits in the late 1980s, they indicated that they were functioning under the protection of other elementals, beings we later came to know as the elves; while they were tolerant of that description, it was clearly inadequate. The old Scandinavian word *elf* is misleading; one might imagine tiny faerylike creatures. But with my inner eye, I saw the elves as slender beings of light, some ten feet tall and very colorful. They had a kind of transparent fluidity and, like a rainbow, were full of radiance.

An inner conversation with these elegant rainbowlike beings informed me that they had been on Earth even before the first plants took shape. In the vastness of time, they had worked to make the entire planet into a garden, with the help of innumerable Nature spirits from the elemental realms and guidance from Angelic beings. Each one continuously contributes something of its own essence to form the natural world and, over an immensity of time, they have together been instru-

Angel, from a painting by Perugino.

mental in forming the rivers and oceans, the valleys and the mountains. They balance cold areas with hot places, creating all the diversity of landscape and climate on Earth, just as the Aborigines of Australia, whose song lines commemorate the original creation of their ancestors, have long believed. So a rugged symmetry has been created between the wild, less hospitable areas of the world and the softer environments more favorable for the development of human and animal life.

It was evident that neither the Nature spirits nor the elves were in a happy state. The Nature spirits were losing the will to maintain the plant life in their care because they themselves were losing energy, and the reason for this appeared to be that the elves were about to depart, leaving this planet for another.

I have to say that my first reaction was, *Oh, no, they are leaving a sinking ship! Why don't they stay and help?*

It was then that I learned that the elves no longer felt able to provide inspiration for the Nature spirits because a part of this planet's evolutionary process required that at a certain stage the responsibility for Earth's maintenance should be handed over to humanity. By now we were expected to have learned to work in effective harmony with Nature and the unseen world that lies behind our own. It seemed, too, to be part of the natural order that the elves should continue their work elsewhere, and so, coming to the end of their allotted time on Earth, they knew they had to leave. Realizing that human sensitivity has tended to diminish rather than increase, this distressed them; our understanding has fallen short of expectations.

The evolutionary life plan for Earth has not been fulfilled because of our insensitivity to the natural world and to each other, and the lack of interaction between people and the Nature spirits. Early humans were more interactive with their natural environment than we are now, but as human activity has developed we have progressively become more enmeshed in matter. The passing of time has seen people become more identified with the physical body, more attached to material possessions, and less aware of Spirit. We have become separated from the spirit within all matter. We were intended to develop an integrated, conscious awareness of life as a whole, but material gain and physical satisfaction have instead become humanity's primary motivation.

As our current religions expanded and became more powerful, their dictates have excluded the recognition of ethereal life forms. Dionysus, Pan, and all spirits of Nature were relegated to folklore, while Angels became the subject of disputes, tolerated but reduced to decorative figures in paintings. Religious institutions took control of people's lives, and their leaders, becoming obsessed with power, declared themselves the necessary intermediaries between the individual and the Creator. Challenges to their authority have led to the persecution of all those "heretics" schooled in the old ways, since personal power and individual forms of belief were not sanctioned. Many thousands were tortured and eliminated by the medieval Inquisition, as well as in religious wars and crusades.

As a result, frightened people gradually forgot how to commune with Nature. The old solar and lunar celebrations were taken over by the new orders and their meanings overlaid with new religious rites; the populace were expected—even compelled—to attend, but as witnesses not as active participants. Needless to say, this has not made our world a better place. People have become disempowered and divorced from their environments, while religious fanaticism and nationalist violence continue to destroy many people's lives.

There are exceptions to this ugly process. A more enlightened awareness has begun to stir in the civilizations of the West. This is also true in the East where, for more than twenty-five hundred years, Buddhism and the Tao, or The Way, have flourished—two philosophies that enable the individual to seek enlightenment without being coerced on the path.

Mainstream orthodoxy based on the exclusive use of the mind, the literal reading of texts, cannot provide solutions to human-created problems. People are looking elsewhere for guidance, and a deep awakening has begun where needed, in the individual. We are searching now for the wisdom of our remote past, way beyond what the current history books teach. We may find essential wisdom in the old ways, this time without fear of persecution and with a more extensive understanding of the greater whole to which we are connected. We are each an integral part of Creation, and so have within us the ability to be conscious creators, true citizens of the world within our own lifetimes.

The human race began to lose its way a long time ago. Accordingly, we have been given teachers at intervals throughout history to remind us of our place in the Universe. As we know, most of them were disposed of by the authorities of the time as troublemakers, and much of their teaching distorted to fit the current orthodoxy when it was realized how popular their simple guidance was. But always there were some who understood the kinder truth of those enlightened beings and kept the knowledge alive, passing it down through the ages and keeping it hidden until the right time for it to be shared.

The elves, however, did not have such teachers; in the beginning, teachers were not needed. But as humans forgot their place in the natural order, so apparently did the elves, followed by the Nature spirits, and it seems now as if they are all looking to humans for help to find it again.

Through my own communion with the elves, I learned that although they had no choice but to depart Earth, they lacked the energy to make the shift to another planet. They saw their departure as the approach of death rather than a transition. Not understanding dying, as they were not part of the earthly cycles of birth and death, the elves were confused and deeply concerned about the fate of the Nature spirits and of the planet itself.

I thought it likely that my experience of the elves' departure was shared with people elsewhere on the planet who were especially sensitive to the natural world. Maybe my home became a focus for them since I could feel their great sorrow and longed to help them. They loved Earth—that exquisite world of trees and plants, birds, animals, fish, and insects—and could see the spreading devastation caused by human neglect and our material and commercial priorities. Before leaving, they had felt it necessary to make a connection with human beings who might be responsive to their plight and to that of the planet. They wanted an assurance that, in future, we would do everything in our power to work with the natural world rather than against it.

So it was that our link with the elves apparently gave them sufficient energy to leave, some going to Jupiter and others to Neptune, where their service would be required in ways that might differ from their functions on Earth. From all over the planet, they seemed to be calling their family together. They gathered over several months and, because they had little enough energy for the journey, some took advantage of human ways of traveling. This led to some amusing incidents, which would sound unbelievable had I not experienced them.

Throughout that summer, a surprising number of friends, returning from holidays abroad, came to visit—each time unknowingly accompanied by groups of elves. It began to feel very crowded. I wished I had a bigger house, perhaps a medieval hall with high rafters, so they did not have to bow their heads beneath our low ceilings! I could sense them stooping low to fit in.

Some had arrived after quite strange journeys. A friend's flight from America was canceled and all the passengers transferred to a larger plane with empty seats; apparently the elves themselves had arranged this, wanting the experience of crossing the Atlantic in a jumbo jet! My friend had first become aware of their presence while walking in Central Park in New York, as with a rustling and swirling of leaves they gathered to join her for the journey. Elves particularly enjoy the company of people with bright auras, so that many came in with the young friends of my children. Throughout the summer they continued to come, leaving again in small groups when they felt ready, but not before communicating with us and passing on information about themselves.

We were told that, in the space of a few years, one of them would return to be born as a human child. This person would have greater spiritual awareness as well as human strengths. They would grow up to work with others to look after the planet, helping to bring about a fuller understanding of Earth's place in the Cosmos, and our own responsibility for it.

Before they left, these elfin spirits gave me an unexpected personal message:

There is something for you to do. We will tell you later what it is; we cannot tell you now.

Then they went; one minute they were there, the next they had vanished. The house seemed incredibly empty. I felt deeply saddened that by not receiving the rest of the information I had failed them in some way.

But a few years later, while walking among the stones at Carnac, I had heard a voice that seemed to come from the oddly shaped Giant, the largest stone in the main alignment, and it said, *This is a library.* I realized then that the work was to be there. I was to listen to the messages in the standing stones, left there by the Angelic realm. I had found what I had to do and had not failed the elves.

Ever since my own interaction with Nature spirits and the elves, I have noticed a major and continuing shift of awareness around me concerning care for the environment. For quite some time, there has been a conscious cooperation with the elementals—in the work of the Findhorn community in Scotland, for example, starting with the successful cultivation of vegetable crops in a difficult soil. This example has led many other people to tend their crops and gardens with the help of the Nature spirits. A parallel phenomenon is emerging in Russia where the rapidly spreading *dachnik* movement has emerged. Small country gardens are kept by city dwellers, similar to the British allotments of wartime, but inspired by the *Anastasia* books in the remarkable *Ringing Cedars* series, now available in many countries and languages.

On a larger scale, there is a gradual spread of organic and biodynamic farming, and new attention is being paid worldwide to caring for the landscape, using sustainable building techniques and improving energy conservation. Scientists research plants and fungi that can regenerate dead soil by absorbing toxins and restoring nutrients. Whether consciously or unconsciously, more people are coming to recognize that there is a life force that keeps us, and our planet, alive. Since the spirits of Nature understand all this much better than we do, we still have much to learn from them. Our survival as a species may well depend on cooperation with them in the future. Our spiritual evolution certainly does.

These beings, normally imperceptible, are all around us. Sometimes I see them, sometimes I do not. I was aware once of water sprites dancing over the waves and accompanying our boat to Fingal's Cave off the holy island of Iona. On the way back, they were not there. Perhaps they stayed in the cave, where the water lapped playfully against the rocks.

Another time I was not enjoying the conversation at a particularly dull dinner party, when something drew my attention to the window, where I could see an ancient oak overlooking the garden. To my surprise and delight, a huge Nature spirit seemed to be perched in the branches, grinning at me. This vision lifted my spirits immediately, making me aware that there was more energy in the garden than among the people around the dinner table. I have a feeling that the elementals tend to make themselves visible to people who would most likely not be frightened to see them, those who are both well grounded in life and yet aware of other dimensions, and who have made a certain amount of inner preparation.

Children are more open to seeing Nature spirits than adults. As a child of four, I climbed the stairs to the attic rooms of our house with the family dog. The dog was as taken aback as I was, when we reached the top step and found the whole landing covered with tiny men dressed in red, wearing the proverbial long pointed hats and shoes, and busily rushing about. As they became aware of our presence they gradually faded away, until the landing was empty again. Although the experience was unexpected, I do not remember thinking it strange, although I have always wondered why they were in the house and not in the garden. I never mentioned it to anyone, and I never saw them again.

According to ancient lore, there are many different kinds of elemental entities, but only some are able, or even have the desire, to work with humans. Those who are willing do so because it seems to be necessary for our development as well as their own. I am certain that such cooperation is essential, not just with Nature spirits but with the elemental and Angelic kingdom as a whole. Angels and other beings have the power to interact with us to transform our lives, and our planet, provided we realize that we cannot do it entirely on our own.

With their cooperation, we can work with the greater consciousness that permeates the Universe. We can gain some understanding of the unseen forces that shape our world, and hence our lives.

3

Carolyn's Journal

I. Tumulus St-Michel – first morning, overcast, windy

I LEFT MY BIKE HIDDEN in the hedges of broom at the base of the tumulus and joined the group of people gathering for a guided tour of the interior. The weather was overcast and windy, and the energies here were strong, making my head throb. I was impatient to be on top but wanted to take the opportunity to go into the belly of the beast before climbing to the summit.

As I entered with the others, I felt the now-familiar pressure in my throat and had to take several shuddering breaths to keep from crying. None of the others seemed to be particularly affected by the strong energies here, and I wondered why. I stayed at the back of the group as we trod a narrow tunnel, lit only by the guide's lantern, to a dolmen of huge proportions completely covered by the packed rocks and earthen rubble of the mound. He shone his light into the passageway, pointing out a granite structure like the dolmen at Kercado, but much larger. We then followed him along a twisting path to several miniscule cells, each too small to fit anything but a child's body. He explained that the path we walked had been bored into the solid core of the mound in 1906 by a French archaeologist. Our guide turned out his lantern for a few moments, and we felt what the excavators must have felt—that they were buried in the Earth itself. The darkness was claustrophobic and the

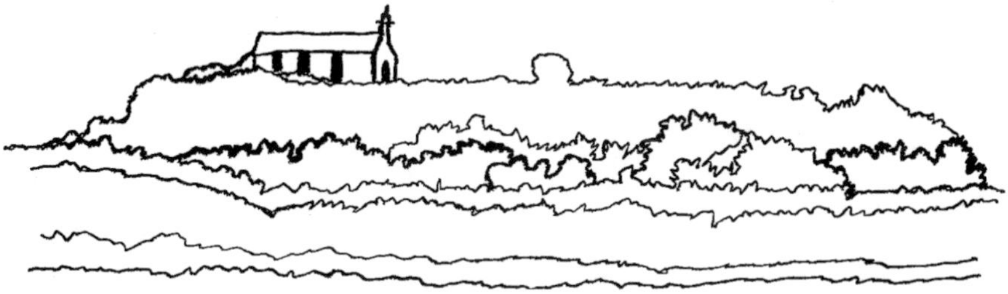

The tumulus and chapel

energy a live thing, pushing and swelling through my body and taking my breath away. I tried not to panic.

Thankfully, we emerged finally into the light and fresh wind of the day and climbed to the top of the tumulus from which the whole countryside—alignments, village, pine woods, ocean, and even my own neighborhood—spread out below us in a grand panorama.

The group followed our guide into the small chapel, but I stayed behind to explore the environs of the summit, settling into a quiet lookout amid sweet-smelling bushes of broom on the side facing Kercado. I located Kercado by the modern water tower peeking out amidst the pine trees, and when I heard my group leave the chapel and start down the tumulus chatting and laughing, I stood up, alone on the summit, and closed my eyes. My two-week meditation had officially begun.

Once I felt centered and quiet, I gazed down on the coast and the alignments, the wind in my face and my mind open to whatever might be there to offer guidance. Drawn to the edge that faced the sea, I looked down upon the town of Carnac, aware that images and words were already beginning to gather in my mind. Journal in hand, I started to take notes:

- *Dolmens and tumuli gather and store energy.*
- *Standing stones receive and transmit energy.*
- *In Nature it is the same: energy is accumulated, stored, then distributed to where it is needed.*
- *In a healthy ecosystem or a healthy body, energy is equitable, balanced, and freely flowing. Call it a "balanced distribution of energy."*
- *In an unhealthy ecosystem or unhealthy body, the energy is stuck and does not flow freely.*
- *Balanced distribution reflects the pattern of the Universe.*
- *Unbalanced distribution is disharmony, dis-ease.*
- *Megalithic structures are ways to balance the distribution of energy, thus maintaining the pattern of the Universe.*

Whew! What a wallop! Dazed, I sat down to read my notes. They had spilled out faster than my hand could write, and the page was covered with an almost indecipherable scrawl of words I only partially understood.

Take your time.

This came as a sensation of sweetness, like a reassuring twinkle in the eye. I wondered if any of the tourists now arriving on top of the tumulus could tell by looking at me that I was receiving messages from an unseen source. Did it show? I took a deep breath and decided, before something else happened, it was time to take a break and go down into town to get something to eat before going on to Le Ménec. But I was not to be given a break just yet.

Simplify your diet: Vegetables, fruit, fish, cheese.

"But I love baguettes!"

Moderation in all things. Enjoy.

Again I felt the twinkle. Whatever was guiding me seemed to have a sense of humor, like a loving relative; the spreading warmth in my chest I identified as gratitude.

Train your intuition and you expand what you recognize as real.

The more intuitive you are, the larger the context of your life.

To know the Universe as a vast, complex, single organism is a function of these stones.

I gazed out at the landscape surrounding the tumulus—land, sea, sky, and stones spreading in every direction—and recognized the seamless wholeness of all of it.

Good. Wholeness is the clue.

Body, mind, heart, spirit perceive Wholeness directly.

Connect always with the Whole.

All a-tremble, I scrambled down to the base of the tumulus, found my bike in the bushes, and excitedly took off down the road toward the village. This was way beyond anything I had ever expected. If Jiri happened to phone tonight, would I tell him what was happening?

Did I even know what was happening? I pedaled down the road alongside the alignments and coasted around the bend toward the village. By the time I had reached the covered market and bought some bread, cheese, and a bag of tomatoes, I knew that it was too soon to speak of this to anybody, even Jiri. Not because he would not understand but because I suspected the teachings had to remain collected and quiet inside me until they was ready to be distributed... just like a dolmen.

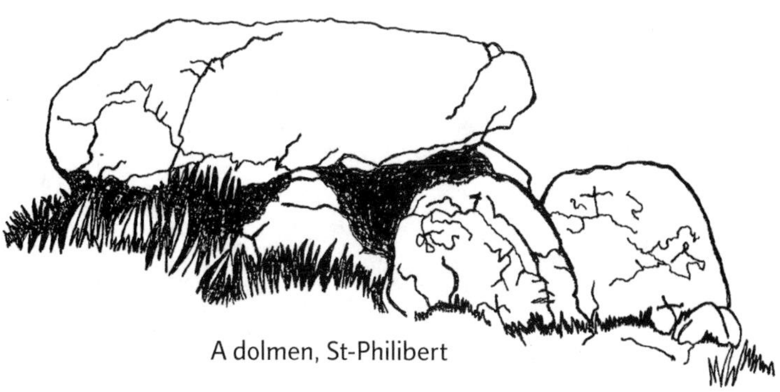

A dolmen, St-Philibert

II. Le Ménec – afternoon, overcast

THE ROW OF STONES farthest in from the road bordered a field where two horses grazed. Starting at the top of that innermost row, I began walking. First I trod the width of the alignments across all twelve rows, then I started down their length, following the lines all the way down to where the stones were only up to my knees, and all but hidden in tall grasses and gorse. Along the way I passed grazing cows, stone cottages, and an occasional tourist taking pictures.

The alignment stones were becoming more familiar to me, feeling more now like old friends from a place I had once lived. One middle-sized stone alongside the pasture was particularly inviting and, as nobody else was around and it was about the right size to climb onto, I hoisted myself up. It had a strong buzz, and I waited to see what might happen.

It did not take long before my body started rocking, so subtly my breath itself seemed to be doing the rocking. I closed my eyes and gradually the radius of the motion grew larger. My shoulders began to lift and my arms followed, shaking themselves out until I was shaking all over. I took a deep breath and cracked open one eye, relieved to note that no tourists were around to witness me bucking like a bronco on my stone horse. I jerkily allowed this odd ride to run its course, and then

Le Ménec, the cromlech

felt a shooting pain, familiar from an old injury, assert itself in my left knee. Not since the bus accident I had been in as a young teenager had I felt this particular tearing and wrenching pain in my knee, and it took me by surprise. The terror of that night flooded back into my whole body and for a while I was right back there, groaning in the turned-over bus with people screaming all around me. Then the scene faded, and the pain shifted to my calf. The ache throbbed hard there, burning like fire before it shifted lower, into my ankle, then bit by-bit spread into my toes. I gasped with the pain until, with a jolt, it passed all the way through, leaving me limp and out of breath. My once-injured leg now dangled loosely over the side of the stone, and I could feel my calf and knee and hip muscles subtly rearranging themselves from where they had settled those many years ago after the bus accident.

And I began to cry. These megaliths were healing stones!

Yes. Listen.

I waited for stillness, and listened.

Face the stone behind you.

I awkwardly shifted on the stone, found a comfortable base and felt the pressure rise in my throat again before the rocking resumed. Almost immediately, old longings surfaced into my chest, spreading into every nook and cranny like heartbreak. There was my childhood recurrent dream of searching through mountains for my people, finding them at a campfire or by a lake, and then losing them again. I slumped over, my forehead touching stone, and sobbed like a baby. Again, I opened one bleary eye to reassure myself that nobody was about and continued to rock back and forth, lulled into a trance.

Face the stone alongside you.

Again I readjusted, found a comfortable base, and felt an ache in my gut, like nausea. My father seemed to be watching me from the branch of a nearby tree and my mother was there, too, out of her mind. I felt them both, smelled their fear and helpless confusion, and every muscle in my body contracted.

Stay with it.

The pain was too excruciating. I slipped into an old pattern of avoidance, trying to look anywhere but there.

Stay with it.

"No!" I screamed silently.

You can.

I buried my mind in sand, muffling a dread almost as old as I was.

Stay with it.

The instructions were gentle but firm and, despite all my resistance, there was no choice but to trust them. I don't know for how long I breathed around that old, debilitating dread, but eventually I felt it dissolve, bit by bit, like butter melting over fire. And then the hurt was a mere shadow, a memory of pain.

I drew in a shaky breath. Opening my eyes and returning to the present from scenes of a child's uncomprehending agony, I was amazed to find myself whole, in a land by the shore of an unfamiliar sea, where tall stones surrounded me like a protecting army. I was not alone here.

I climbed down unsteadily and lay on the ground to recover. I must have slept—a sweet, protected rest on ferns and grass warmed by the sun. I awoke feeling drained but calm and ready again for whatever came. I felt my body against the Earth, body and Earth breathing together, perfectly synchronized.

Observe.

My body, *the* human body, asserted itself in my mind. I felt my own as a template for all human bodies, with torso and head, symmetrical limbs, spinal chord, and vital systems in continuous, interconnected motion, alive. Onto this body appeared a pattern of needles, like the acupuncture needles Chinese healers use. Each little pin touched into an invisible stream of energy just beneath the skin, which circulated all through the body. I could feel the stream flowing. My body seemed to grow larger and larger, until it was as big as the Earth. Then I saw the needles thickening into needles of stone. Oh!

The Earth has a subtle energy system, too.

I let that sink in. It made sense—the Earth a macrocosm and the body a microcosm. We were essentially the same thing, planets and people.

Everything is connected. Everything is related.

Slowly, I sat up. Still light-headed, I looked around me at stones and grass, sky above and the Earth below, my own self seated in between them. A bird sailed above and settled in the branch of the tree, not far from where I had imagined my father watching me. She pecked at the branch, then flew off. I followed her flight and felt my hand against the ground, wondering. I could sense an intelligence waiting for me to ask the next question. And then it came:

If acupuncture needles in the human body are activated by the acupuncturist, then who activates the stones?

Who do you think?

It had to be us, the humans.

III. Kercado – early evening, clear

I MANAGED TO GET hopelessly lost in the maze of the town dump, trying to find Kercado. One path after another led through the garbage, only to dead-end in a pile of trash, so I finally gave it up as a lost cause. I was very tired and so over-stimulated by the day's revelations that I decided to just go home. Tomorrow I would come on foot and find the trail that Jiri and I had followed up to Kercado.

Of course, as soon as I was coasting down the hill on my bike toward Kerfraval, I found the paved road that led to the unpaved road, that became the narrow trail that turned into the footpath, that led to where the passage mound and dolmen called Kercado had been placed almost 5,000 years before Christ.

Memorizing the landmarks so I could find it again, I deliberately did not give in to the temptation to take a peek, but followed the road back down the hill toward the Briard house, looking forward to a long hot bath, supper at the café, and some relaxed hours on the beach reading about magnetism at neolithic stone sites.

The Kercado menhir

IV. Early next morning, clear

THE NEXT MORNING I brought my portable tape recorder with me. I wanted to start each day dancing, as a way of warming up my body and being as receptive as possible to whatever might come through. Warming up with dancing had been my morning meditation for quite a while by this time, and I wondered how doing it at the stones would feel. Now, the tape recorder was in my backpack as I pedaled up the hill, finding my way to the paved road that turned into the unpaved road. I got off my bike and walked the grassy trail to the footpath that led to the site.

I left my bike leaning against a tree, then stepped reverently into the grove surrounding the mound, wondering if it would look different to me in the morning light, if it would *know* me. A bit tremulously, I moved into the clearing and was immediately disoriented; there was no mound. Where was I? Nothing looked familiar. Had I come to the wrong place? I felt a moment of vertigo before realizing that I was facing in the wrong direction and turned around, laughing out loud at myself. Reorienting, I found everything back where it was supposed to be. I walked around the mound clockwise toward the opening, which today was closed off, its makeshift wooden door locked shut.

I was alone there—no surprise at this hour—and I made a second circuit of the mound, my eyes on the standing stone on its crown. She was mute and innocent in the morning sunlight. On my third time around, I searched the grass for evidence that Jiri and I had really been here on the night of the full moon, needing to be sure I had not made this whole drama up. I found my proof at the edge of the meadow, where some burnt blades of grass indicated the spot our campfire had been. I knelt and felt around, fingering a bit of charred twig, some cold embers. We *had* been here; I had actual history with this place.

I put my tape recorder down, turned it on, and danced to African rhythms, shaking out my arms and legs, bending my spine and torso, and getting my pelvis into motion with shimmies and thrusts. Soon I was breathing deeply and evenly, my body awake, my mind calm. I was ready to start the day. Luxuriously, I shook myself out one last time, turned off the tape recorder, and looked around.

I was not alone. A pure white cat lay on the grass by the dolmen and watched me with yellow eyes that followed my every gesture. I walked over, squatted down to her level, and stretched out my hand.

"Who are you, *petit chat*?" She rose to nuzzle her head against the back of my hand, purring.

"Are you the gatekeeper, or my familiar?" She rubbed her whiskers against my arm and flopped over, inviting me to pet her furry belly. "Or maybe you are just

a little cat?" She allowed me to stroke her just long enough to let me know I was welcome, then sprang up, tail high in the air, and stalked out of sight. When she had disappeared into the wood I went over to the tall menhir opposite the entrance to the chamber, the stone Jiri had sat against on the night of the full moon. I sat where he had sat, its well-placed bump supporting me at heart level as it must have done for him. I felt a steady pulsing entering my back.

Masculine.

The sensation was of male energy.

From the stone atop the mound I felt something enter my chest, more like a gentle, spreading pulse.

Feminine.

Both were felt qualities rather than verbal cues, but moments later a word sprang into my mind.

Balance.

The sun was warm through the pinewood, and birds flitted across the clearing, their wingbeats and burbles constituting the sounds of the morning. All around me the site felt peaceful, in balance. I imagined Jiri here, exactly where I sat now. His body must have breathed against this stone, just as I was breathing now, the air of the world becoming his body's air, and now my air, cell by cell, organ by organ.

I inhaled and exhaled, and the world entered me, circulated, was used, released, and changed. Balanced distribution.

As I observed myself breathing, my mind was also sparking with insights and impressions, circulating them just like the air. I picked up my journal and started a list as ideas occurred to me:

- Standing stones receive and transmit energy from above and below.
- Energy steps down and is transformed by alignments and stone circles
- Mounds and dolmens and tumuli gather and store this energy.
- Masculine energy and feminine energy must be harmonized and

distributed in a balanced way for life to be maintained.
- I have no idea what "energy" means, except that I sense that everything comes from it, that it connects everything to everything else...

Here I came to the limits of what I understood.

Breathe.

I breathed. Rising to my feet, I went looking for the cat. I wanted to tell someone what I had just learned, but she wasn't in sight. Instead, I climbed up the mound and put my arms around the standing stone there in a scratchy hug, remembering how we had danced together by the full moon just a week earlier. Then I searched for a place to sit in the welter of thorny brambles growing out of her base.

"You're a lot more prickly than the masculine stone below you," I told her in a murmur.

We take turns.

It felt like we were sharing a joke. Me and a very old stone. I was losing my mind, for sure.

Take dictation.

I opened my journal to a clean page and, pen in hand, sat waiting. Crazy or not, this could hardly be more intriguing.

Love is the constant Wholeness.

Love is the Source.

Love is the unheard hum of the Universe.

This time I received the message in words. I wrote them down, word for word.

The megaliths tap into the love field and transmit energies for all the forms of the world.

Now my own mind took over. I wrote as quickly as my hand could get the words down on paper:

It's transformation; that's the key! In this whole process, the energy gets synthesized, changed in some way—just like food metabolism in the body: it is eaten in one form, released as energy in another form. In being used, it becomes something else.

There is a background of motion and change—that's a given, that's Nature. What we do is to lightly tap into it, placing specific intention and specific activity upon the natural state of things.

And what is this given state but Love, no matter where we are or when we live? So I find myself the woman I am, right here at Kercado, on this day in 1984, but I could be anyone, anywhere, any time, adoring this child, that man, that woman.

The adoring is the constant—love is already there, no matter where the "there" is, no matter when.

As I read over what I had written, my hand continued writing—this time not my own words:

The most important question is, what is the ultimate Nature of Reality?

To understand the form and function of anything in the world—these stones included—you must ask the larger question, otherwise nothing makes any sense.

The ultimate Nature of what is real informs every single thing in the world.

The cat emerged from the trees and made her way unhesitatingly towards the mound. Lightly, she leapt up, trotted to where I sat, and draped herself on my lap, kneading my thigh with a velvet paw. I stroked and stroked her warm body, not sure whether she was in my imagination or actually on my lap.

V. Kerlescan – afternoon, sunny and breezy

A TOUR BUS stood idling noisily at the Le Ménec alignments when I cycled up, so I kept on going down the road. I passed the alignments at Kermario, a mile up the road, and kept going until I arrived at Kerlescan, the farthest and wildest section of the Carnac alignments. Kerlescan means "the burning place," and I wondered at what point in history it got that name, and why? The woods were thick here, the energies strong, and the stones, although obscured by the profuse vegetation around them, immense.

I noticed, after almost two weeks of being around megaliths, that my body was adjusting more easily to their energies, and I was feeling generally more attuned to them. They were more accessible—but only if I slowed down. I had begun learning how to move at a different pace and how to practice a new kind of attentiveness—a slow attentiveness... appropriate to standing stones.

Right now I was alone here at this peaceful and rarely visited section of the alignments. The sky stretched blue in every direction, and the buzz of insects filled the fragrant air. I leaned against one stone, resting and allowing my body to absorb its distinctive quality. Then I shifted to another, sensing a subtle difference. Then I went back to the first stone. Just at the edge of awareness, I felt the slightest hum registering on my skin, as if the "note" of this stone was a different pitch than the other. Eyes closed, I went back and forth between the two stones, hearing them, feeling the difference their subtle vibrations made on my skin. I listened and tried to hum with each stone, back and forth, back and forth. Then I went to a third stone, excited by my discovery.

Vibration is sound, is heat, is color, is matter, is form.

Kerlescan menhir

The message came as words and images combined. I opened my eyes to ponder this, gazing into the middle distance, totally absorbed in my own thoughts. Then a flash of red amid the granite grays and greens of the stone rows caught me up short, and I immediately froze. My trance rudely broken, I recalled the badly crippled man I had passed on the road on my way here, who had leered provocatively at me as I cycled by, gesturing toward the dark woods with his crutch. He had been wearing a red sweater just this color. I clutched with fear when he limped into view from around the stones.

"*Bonjour,*" he greeted in a gravelly voice. I backed away.

"*Bonjour,*" I replied, backing away some more. "Wonderful, these stones," I added brightly, as if it were the most normal thing for him to find me alone in this place where, it seemed, nobody ever came. He limped closer. "Do you live around here?" I asked.

"Over there," he replied, "*là-bas,*" gesturing towards the woods on the other side of the road. He was just a local fellow, I chastised myself—a lonely, crippled man who wanted some company. What was I being so paranoid about? Wasn't I supposed to be a healer?

"Are you in pain?" I asked, professionally.

"Always," he replied, coughing hoarsely.

"These are healing stones, you know."

"They haven't healed *me,*" he grumbled, his eyes shifting back and forth.

"How did this happen to you?" I heard myself asking, as if I were a nurse taking his history.

He hung his head, and after a lengthy silence told me about the harvesting machine that had turned over on him ten years ago on his farm. He had nearly died, and it had scarred his face as well as his body, he said, making him look like a monster. He was not exaggerating. My heart went out to him, and I decided not to be such a ninny.

"These stones may be able to help you," I offered. "I know a way that might be able to take away some of your pain. Would you be willing?"

The longing in his eyes broke my heart, and I chose a stone right by the road and waited for him to join me there. When he pointed his crutch toward the stones far from the road instead, I had second thoughts. Maybe I should just grab my bike and get out of there. Again I chastised myself; it wasn't as if I couldn't outrun him if necessary.

"Here," I insisted, placing my hand on the roadside stone. For a moment he held his ground, but I did the same, and eventually he dragged himself over to where I stood. I kneeled out of reach of his grasp and placed my hands on his ankles. The pain was palpable.

Focusing, I visualized the congestion dissolving and the energy flowing freely. I kept my head bowed and my eyes closed in concentration until I felt a regular pulse in his poor wasted ankle joints. Once I could sense energy moving in his lower legs, I glanced up to ask how he was feeling, but what I encountered was an erect penis sticking out of his pants.

"Kiss me!" he begged, as I jumped to my feet and started to run away. "*Embrasse moi!*"

"Mais monsieur, I cannot," I called back to him, as I flung a leg over my bike seat and took off in a hurry, "I'm a married woman!" And pedaling as fast as I could, I headed back toward Le Ménec and the safety of a busload of tourists.

In the morning, a Goddess cat; in the afternoon, a sad, nightmare man. What was I likely to encounter at the tumulus when I got there later?

VI. Tumulus St-Michel – late afternoon, clear

THE FEW PEOPLE still around when I arrived on top of the tumulus were on their way down, so I had the little chapel to myself. Bach was playing on a gramophone and, still shaken by my encounter at Kerlescan, I curled up in a corner of the sanctuary and let myself be comforted by the chapel's protecting walls and the familiar harmonies of a Bach chorale.

To heal, reinstate harmony where harmony has been lost.

With the Bach, I felt my body absorb this message, and my breathing calmed down. With each chord of the music, my tension dissolved, until I was half-asleep on the floor.

To heal, re-tune all parts of the body with each other, and re-tune the body with the Earth.

The flute duet from Bach's *Sheep May Safely Graze* floated into the little chapel, and I relaxed with gratitude into it, humming along with this well-loved melody.

Healing. Wholeness. Holiness. Three words, one meaning.

Comforted, I took in both music and message, feeling my spirit lift and my heart open.

That's it. Memorize the feeling.

What I felt was a kind of weightless ease, a gladness to be right here, right now; a joy in the sounds of the music, a delight in my adventure with all its unexpected twists and turns, a rush of gratitude to have been given this opportunity to be in Brittany at the megaliths.

Good.

And then came the image of a rimless wheel with spokes radiating in all directions like a shining star. Everything in the whole world was on the wheel, and the wheel was turning—had always been turning—all parts in endless relation to every other part. Nothing stayed the same, everything changed constantly, but the whole wheel appeared absolutely still. It was a stillness that contained all motion, glorious in its perfection. While the vision remained, I was caught in a kind of rapture. Slowly, it faded.

See?

"Yes," I breathed, then I thought about the man in the red sweater. How did his pain and my fear of him fit in?

He is part of the Whole, just as everything is. That includes pain and evil and fear.

I took that in.

Listen.

Bach's B Minor Mass filled the chapel. I listened with eyes closed. The music entered my body like light-tipped arrows, and my breathing slowed as I drifted toward sleep.

Stay alert.

My head cleared, and I sat up against the chapel wall, my legs straight out and my toes keeping rhythm with Bach. I entered a state of calm attention in which my mind and body both grew still. I was as relaxed as I had ever been, but also as clearly conscious as I had ever been.

The information continued to tumble through me. In my mind's eye, I saw living systems in dynamic interaction with each other, swirling through every dimension in time and space. Everything, visible and invisible, interacted with everything else, always in motion, always in transformation.

I saw how Earth, Air, Fire, and Water perfectly balanced each other, emerging continuously from an invisible, all-encompassing, subtle matrix that was conscious but not human. I felt it as a force holding together every single thing in existence; it was an irresistible pull of attraction. It was Love. The vision held long enough for me to fix it in my awareness, but not long enough for me to write it down.

I could feel it profoundly but not describe it. No words. The words that came to mind—some in English, some in French—were too limited to describe the ecstatic, alive, many-faceted images I was receiving. Only now, more than twenty years later, am I able to attempt translating those perceptions into language.

I recognized then that nothing exists outside the context of the whole, and that everything in the world is in relationship with everything else in the world, throughout all of time and space and beyond.

Bach knew this, too—I could hear it in his music.

The whole Universe is conscious. Every stone, every wind.

Bemused, I let that sink in, visualizing the consciousness of stone, of air, of water. I drifted with the images again. I must have fallen into a doze because I was awakened by a kindly caretaker who bent over me with a concerned expression on his face. It was closing time, he told me softly. Flustered, I took a moment to orient myself. Then, apologizing, I picked myself up off the floor, smoothed down my hair and, with as much dignity as I was able to muster, left the chapel to stumble down the side of the tumulus to where my bike was waiting in the bushes.

VII. Kercado – morning, clear and still

I ENTERED THE GROVE in the stillness of early morning; the grass atop the mound was wet with dew and still in shade when I climbed up to the menhir on top. It welcomed me, and I leaned my back against it, waiting for the sun to warm us. Last night it had rained. The air was fresh, the trees and grass dewy and green. This time the makeshift wooden door to the chamber stood open and the energies that emanated felt benign.

Enter the chamber.

I felt this as a downward tug and an image of the darkness inside. Now that I was learning to interpret subtle cues, the message was unmistakable. How much was I still missing, I wondered?

Some. Not too much.

Obediently, I walked down the mound and crouched, crawling into the passageway to the chamber. Leaving the fresh light of the morning felt like entering the underworld, the chamber was that dark and dank. I lowered myself against an upright stone and plunked down, crossing my legs in a meditative posture but try as I might, I could not concentrate. The darkness frightened me, and I didn't want to be alone. The last time I'd been here was with Jiri, and I wished he were here with me now. We had sung here together for the first time, testing our voices and playing with the echoes they raised, bringing our liveliness into the darkness after a strange night of revelations.

Was it only ten days ago? Already I was nostalgic with memories. I hummed into the darkness—my voice vibrating in my belly, then in my chest. The chamber sang the sounds back to me. Bit by bit, my throat opened and my voice warmed. I was singing the flute melody from *Sheep May Safely Graze*, a few notes ringing like bells off the granite slabs of the chamber. The song gradually morphed into an improvisation, in which I played with the resonant notes that rang the space, singing octaves and fifths, listening for overtones and undertones and enjoying myself tremendously.

The improvisation spun into microtones and trills, my voice getting freer with every breath, and softer, until the song eventually rounded to a close. Feeling replete, I sat in the pulsating stillness, completely relaxed, my spine straight and easy, my knees offering no resistance, and my breaths deep and even. I could have sat there forever.

Come up.

I didn't want to leave, but reluctantly I uncrossed my legs and crawled back out the chamber, blinking in the bright light of day. Making my way back up the mound, I sat down again by the menhir and sank back into the sweet sense of repletion I had found down below.

For how long I sat there I do not know, but the sound of human voices close by, and the click of a camera's shutter roused me. My eyes blinked open to the grove in sunlight and to a gray-haired couple nearby, guidebook and camera in hand.

"Hello," they addressed me in Australian-accented English, "we do not speak French."

"Mine isn't very good, either," I admitted, standing up to stretch.

"Then this is not your property?" they asked. I came down off the mound and assured them that I was not the owner of this place; they were as welcome here as

The Kercado dolmen

I was. We shook hands, and they began to inform me of their travels and all the other prehistoric sites they had visited.

"We travel all over the world. This year it's the British Isles and France," the woman told me. I was impressed. She named sites in Ireland they had visited, counting them off on her fingers. Her husband made his way around the mound, snapping pictures. I greeted him when he reached us.

I thought to ask them about Newgrange in Ireland, but the wife wouldn't stop talking; I couldn't have gotten a word in edgewise if I tried! Then they both started talking, telling me about where they had gone, who they had met, what they had seen, the pictures they had taken. In moments, my deep calm had dissolved into smatters of irritation, then downright anger. With dismay, I felt my temper flare way out of proportion to what was actually happening.

Notice.

I kept my anger under control until they left, then I went wild! I stomped all around the grove, kicking rocks and punching the trunks of pine trees, muttering out loud and occasionally yelling in fury. Memories from childhood surfaced one by one.

Notice.

My body remembered words being cut off, feelings ignored, creativity discouraged. This territory was too familiar, and it went deep. I noticed my teeth clenching, my throat tightening.

Breathe.

I breathed. This was bizarre, and I prayed nobody would arrive and witness me, a middle-aged American woman having a fit on a French hillside—and I started to laugh.

Stay with the anger.

I hauled in a shaky breath. The anger surged again, swirling like a red-hot thing in my chest, choking me.

Forgive yourself. Breathe.

I breathed, knowing that self-forgiveness would come eventually, but not yet. The reservoir of childhood impotence that these two talky folks from Australia had sparked still had to be dealt with.

Patience.

I marveled at the unexpected turn the day had taken. It was only noon. What next? My stomach made a bid for lunch, growling with hunger for one of those delicious crêpes with melted cheese they made down at the market. Brushing off the seat of my pants, I braided my hair, shrugged into my backpack and left Kercado, impatient for that first bite of crispy pancake filled with smelly, hot cheese.

VIII. Le Ménec – late afternoon, scattered clouds

AT THE VERY TOP of the Le Ménec alignments, a tiny hamlet is tucked inside what still remains of the stone circle, or *cromlech*, Breton for a protective ring of close-set stones. A cottage in the hamlet contained a shop selling hard cider to those of us who had a thirst, presided over by the elderly lady who lived there. Her bright eyes twinkled with kindly irony as she regarded the stream of researchers who had come through her door over the years, and they twinkled at me as well.

She had been born right here in this house, she told me, had married and raised her children here, and opened up the cottage to visitors only after her husband's death. When I asked her what it was like to live all her life in the midst of the megaliths, she shrugged and replied that it was the only life she knew. Her cider, in fact, was delicious.

"Tell me," she asked encouragingly, "what is your theory about the stones? Everyone who comes here has a theory, so you must have one too, eh?"

A bit of encouragement was all I needed, so I began to tell her some of my latest thoughts. I warmed to my subject, speaking in inadequate French about subtle energies flowing through the Earth, just as they did in our bodies, about invisible realms and interconnected systems—all I had begun to learn since arriving here. Then I ran out of words. She watched me, her eyes crinkling, her smile growing broader. We both burst out laughing.

"And there's another theory!" she observed matter-of-factly. She slapped her thigh with the flat of her hand and filled my glass again. "Everyone has a theory, *n'est pas*? But nobody knows."

"Nobody but the stones," I retorted with a grin, drinking the last sweet drops in my glass and wishing her well before going back out to the alignments.

Rest.

I was ready again for solitude, so I made my way across the rows of stones to the pasture where the foals grazed. Finding an isolated patch of grass, I lay down for a nap. The brown foal came to the fence and kept me company, breathing a soft, rhythmic fuffle in my ears. Together, we inhaled and exhaled while the Earth breathed us. I fell into the deep sleep of someone who has run many miles without stopping—lightened, emptied, and slightly out of breath. When I awoke the foal was gone, and the air had the chill of an impending rain. Just a hint of my dream lingered—twin lambs on a shore at the edge of the waves, the feel of their nubbly wool coats, their tinny bleats in my ears.

When I arrived back at Kerfraval, Madame Briard anxiously awaited me in the kitchen.

"Have you eaten yet?" she asked right away. I never took meals with the family, so I had no idea why she was asking. "Because, my neighbor…" The story was that her friend across the way had heard about the healing of little Pierre's cough and had asked if I would heal her as well.

"I am really not qualified," I protested. "With Pierre, it was just one of those lucky things, and no, I have not eaten yet."

But Madame Briard was not to be dissuaded. Her neighbor had been suffering "down below" for years, she said, and was afraid to go to the doctor. If I would be so kind, the woman would be glad to pay me. She was at home, waiting to be told when to come over.

What to do? Despite my misgivings, I nodded that I would see her.

Madame Briard sat me down at the family table and fed me a bowl of soup before rushing out to tell her neighbor. I felt like an impostor hoisted on her own petard.

Come into concentration and simply be a channel.

Do not try and heal.

That was good advice because the woman put herself into my hands with complete, although unwarranted, trust. Lying right down on my bed, she pulled off her panties and there, all but spilling onto my quilt was a prolapsed uterus that, even if I had wanted to, I could not have fixed. She was quivering. I was, too, but I placed my hands upon her abdomen and simply sat with her. I could feel heat pulse into the crown of my head and, with each breath, pour into my hands.

No ideas. Be simple. It was hard not to pray for her, but my instructions were clear, and each time I started to think in any way about her condition, the instructions were repeated.

Be a channel. Do not try to heal.

I stayed there, my hands lightly on her body, and my mind relaxed and fell into a lovely drowse. I think both of us were snoring softly for a while. When my head lifted of its own accord, I sensed it was time to stop. She opened her eyes, and we exchanged a sweet smile.

"I feel better," she whispered.

"Will you go to the doctor?" I asked.

"Should I?"

"Yes."

By the next day, the word had gotten around the neighborhood that the American healer at the Briard's house was available for free. From that night on, no matter how much I protested, neighbors from up and down the street were watching through their windows for my return home.

4

Natasha

Le Petit Ménec and the Venus Connection

AN OLD GUIDEBOOK DESCRIBES the alignments of Le Petit Ménec as "forgotten" and the area around them as "swampy." Not today. Although separated by a road from the longest rows, which form the three main Carnac alignments, they are signposted now and just visible within their hiding place in the trees. On a recent visit, we found they had been cleared of thick undergrowth.

Happily, the loss of some of their previous romantic setting has not made the stones feel any less magical. After a few paces, a path leads to the remaining stones, set out in a fan shape, with seven or eight rows in some places and, in others, just three. These stones are smaller than those in the main alignments, around shoulder height, many still standing and others fallen.

In the nineteenth century, hundreds of stones were removed to build the lighthouse at Belle-Île. This is rather ironic as they are something of a light-emitting source themselves, quietly giving out a rather different frequency of radiance from their woodland setting.

The first time we arrived at Le Petit Ménec, we felt it to be the most romantic of the many megalithic sites in the area. The summer leaves were speckled with warm sunlight filtering through the trees overhead. It seemed the kind of enchanted place where one might imagine the faery folk lived, those gentle beings who exist in another dimension from our own.

It was here in these surviving stone rows that we discovered, quite by chance, a working gateway to a different realm. Meandering on the footpath, I passed between two upright stones slightly taller than the others, and immediately felt something at waist level pulling me backward. I stepped back in surprise, then repeated the exercise to see if it would happen again. It did—several times. We wondered if this might indeed be some kind of gateway, popularly known as a "portal," and sat quietly musing among the trees, a powerful silence settling all around us like a cloak.

Le Petit Ménec

Not receiving any inner message to explain what had happened, we used a pendulum to ask questions of the guardians of the site, who we felt were well aware of our presence. The answers we received indicated that we had indeed found a portal, and we were being allowed to become familiar with its function as a doorway or link between planet Earth and Venus, for use by Venusian beings who still travel back and forth between those worlds. Perhaps some of them were actually with us in the woods because the energy we felt was both intense yet delightful.

I have a memory from when I was about age nine. One evening, I was gazing with intense fascination at the brightest star in the sky, not understanding then that it was Venus but feeling a strong connection with this light. Astrologically, Venus is, in fact, my ruling planet. It's not surprising, then, that while I was at this portal in France, I experienced a kind of bonding with its vibrations.

It's been said that there are numerous portals scattered across the planet, providing a link to Venus as well as other planets of the solar system. England appears to have several portals that are more recent introductions along energy lines, or ley lines, but others have been there for millennia.

We found two portals in the main Carnac alignments by following our hunches. One is at the western end of the Le Ménec alignment, where a hamlet lies within the *cromlech.* The portal lies inside an old barnlike house that has been unwittingly built over it, and which now serves as a *crêperie*, the place where Carolyn drank cider. Unfortunately, it was always closed when we were there. The other portal lies within the Kerlescan *cromlech.*

Pythagoras, the Greek philosopher and mathematician, recognized the planets as aspects of divine consciousness. He and his followers especially revered Venus because, other than the sun and moon, it is the only celestial object whose light is bright enough to cast a shadow on Earth. At different times of year, it is visible as the morning star just before sunrise, or as our evening star just after sunset—its radiance earning the name Lucifer, the light-bringer.

It brings us spiritual light, also, and is aptly named "Mother of the Gods." The female deities associated with Venus are all goddesses of love: Astarte, Ishtar, Aphrodite, Freya, and, of course, the Egyptian Isis, whose story and iconography of mother and child are parallel to the Christian Mary. Isis was mother of Horus, and Mary was mother of Jesus; in each case, it was the son who brought the essential message of love and wisdom to the people of Earth from a higher source.

Isis and child, Musée Champollion, Figeac

This is similar to other teachers, reputed to be solar gods and sometimes referred to as the "sons, or suns, of the morning star." In the Bible, in the Book of Revelations, Jesus says: "I am the root and the offspring of David, the bright and morning star."

Other ancient spiritual teachings tell us that all the great teachers, in their different guises, are aspects of a single greater consciousness, incarnating on Earth at different times in order to raise the consciousness of the planet and its inhabitants; it is evident that such reminders are still necessary.

It is said that Venus is where human souls return to their origin after many lifetimes on Earth, when they have sufficiently evolved to embody the perfect harmony of Love, the mystical marriage of male and female. American Indian traditions and other legends of the world speak of certain beings coming to Earth from Venus at some past time in order to populate our planet. As beings of light, they were guided by those greater beings of light that we call Angels; they had no need of mechanical conveyances to bring them through the solar system. At that time, they could adapt to conditions on our planet, which they found hospitable. During the ages they remained on Earth, they and the planet evolved together, until they could not so readily come and go except by making use of the portals that provided passageways between the spheres. It would seem from my own experiences that this is still the case.

Only slightly smaller than Earth, and the second of the inner planets from the sun, Venus has always been of great significance to early civilizations on this planet. Quite recently, we have learned from the European Space Agency's Venus Express space probe, a follow-up mission from ESA's Mars Express, that the atmosphere on Venus was once similar to Earth's and, consequently, may have been able to support life, but extreme global warming irrevocably changed conditions. What lesson might we take from that?

The Mayans corrected their calendar by observations of the eight-year Venus cycle, and so a number of the great temple sites in Central America were set up as observatories partially for that purpose. There are other well-known examples, such as the tumulus of Bryn Celli Ddu on Anglesey Island in North Wales, where the light of a rising Venus enters once during each cycle. Like the winter solstice sunrise, to which so many such ancient structures around the world are oriented, Venus was a symbol of rebirth and renewal for the megalithic people. They, too, were accustomed to observe its regular cycles, one of which, as we know from astronomy, traces out a five-pointed star or pentagram in the sky over the eight-year period.

Of the various symbols used to represent Venus, the five-pointed star as a symbol of the feminine is perhaps the most familiar. If you cut an apple in half, through

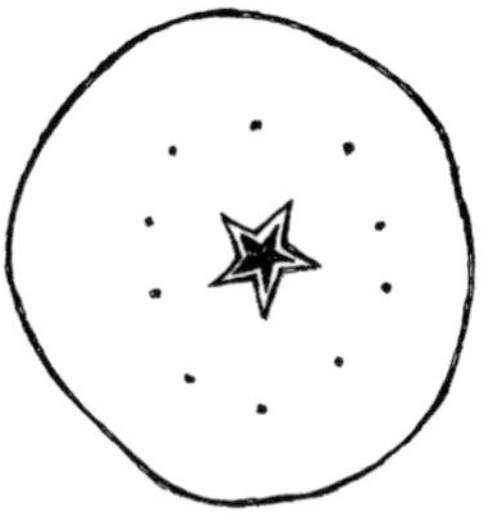

Apple-star

its roundest part, you will find such a star. The apple has, therefore, become a symbol for the beautiful planet that transmits love to the Earth.

Unlike most of the other planetary orbits in the solar system, which are elliptical, the Venus orbit is almost circular and has long been seen as a symbol of harmony. Interestingly, the Venus day is exactly two-thirds of our earthly year, which, in musical terms, is a "fifth indicating consonant harmony." In addition, each time Venus passes between Earth and the sun, we see her same face, just as we always see the same face of our moon. Earth and Venus are, therefore, linked in several harmonious ways: mathematically, musically, and spiritually.

Medieval knights in shining armor, preparing to defend their chosen lady, honored the feminine principle. King Arthur's twelve knights sat at a round table, symbolic of the feminine circle of Venus. It is also interesting to find the Arthurian legends alive and well in Brittany, in the forest of Brocéliande, for instance, where they are associated with megaliths, just as they are in Britain. That's not so surprising when you consider that the Celts migrated to Brittany during the Arthurian period to escape Anglo-Saxon and Danish incursions. The name Brittany, in fact, means "Little Britain."

The custom of eating fish in place of meat on the fifth day of the week, Friday (from the Scandinavian "Freya's day" or *Vendredi* in French, both referring to Venus), was a continuation of the pagan practice of eating fish on that day to revere Venus. Freya is the Scandinavian name for Venus, and the fish was seen as sacred to her, while Isis, the Egyptian goddess, is often shown with a fish in her headdress as well as horns.

Friday is also the Muslim holy day. It is rumored that, at Mecca, the *Kaaba*, the hidden stone toward which Muslims pray, has a Venus symbol carved into it in the shape of a crescent. At the time of the Prophet Mohammad, the female principle was well respected in Islam, as it was in many traditions before patriarchy came to dominate the world scene in both religion and politics.

The *Kaaba* at Mecca is sited on an important energy or ley line, at the former location of a pagan temple where, it seems, tribute was paid to both male and female deities. The Prophet Mohammad is associated with the color green, so those who have made the pilgrimage to Mecca wear green turbans. In the chakra system, green is the color of the fourth or heart chakra, through which love flows, and as the predominant color of the Earth mother, it symbolizes the growth cycles of Nature upon our planet. It is reminiscent, too, of the Green Man, the pagan figure so often seen in medieval church carvings in Europe, and in India, peering out of a halo of leaves with luxuriant foliage growing from his mouth. While the significance of the Green Man has not been entirely understood, if he is seen as Pan, the god of Nature, he may well represent the cycle of green growth and the perennial renewal of life. He would be partner to Gaia, the Earth Mother who is earthly sister to Venus, Mother of the Gods.

It is apparent, therefore, that the planet Venus has long been a vital link in the story of human development and, after a long absence in our world, the old goddesses who represent her qualities of order, love, and harmony, are slowly returning, gathering power to again influence human society.

As the Russian geologist Vernadsky wrote:

> Only man transgresses the established order... upsets the equilibrium, though whether he materially cripples the transforming mechanism [the cosmic energies], or merely redistributes it, we cannot at the moment be sure.

When humanity relearns how to consciously attune and work with cosmic energies in a spirit of true integrity, the Earth will become a radiant light in the Heavens and shine out as brightly as does lovely Venus.

5

Carolyn's Journal

I. Le Manio - morning, storm threatening

THE DAY DAWNED DARK, just like my mood. My period, like the weather, was about to break. I was too restless to stay in bed, so I threw on warm clothes and went out to have an adventure before the weather drove me indoors. My mood was mutinous: whatever made good sense was not on my agenda, and I was looking for trouble. I got this way sometimes when my menses were imminent. I had learned that what suited me best was to give in to it and do something rash right away, so I could spend the rest of the day regretting it in the comfort of a warm bed. Today, rather than going to any of my three sites, I would go in search of Le Manio, the single standing stone which, I was told, stood by itself in the woods on the same side of the road from the alignments.

The air smelled of the coming rain when I took off, and it felt good to push hard up the hill on my bike. Not another soul was out near the alignments, which were shrouded in a layer of mist that obscured them, and I felt as if I were moving back into dreamtime. I steered my bike toward the woods and ducked into the trees where it was even more shadowy, and found the hint of a meandering path in the half-dark. This fit my state of mind perfectly. Shivering with something close to pleasurable anticipation, I propped my bike against a pine tree and continued on by foot, wondering about this strange woman I became during my menstrual periods.

Even so, the Manio giant, when it suddenly appeared in a small clearing, took me by surprise. It was huge. Its presence commanded the whole area, dwarfing me. Even at a distance, I could feel its strong pull and it drew me to it like a magnet attracting a lodestar. Soon I was leaning into its bulk, my ear against granite. I could feel its sound rumble in my chest, and I responded by stretching my arms around it in an embrace. The familiar pressure surged into my throat until, before I knew what was happening, huge, shaking sobs were coming out of me as if my heart would break. The grief was irresistible, nor did I have any inclination to stop the

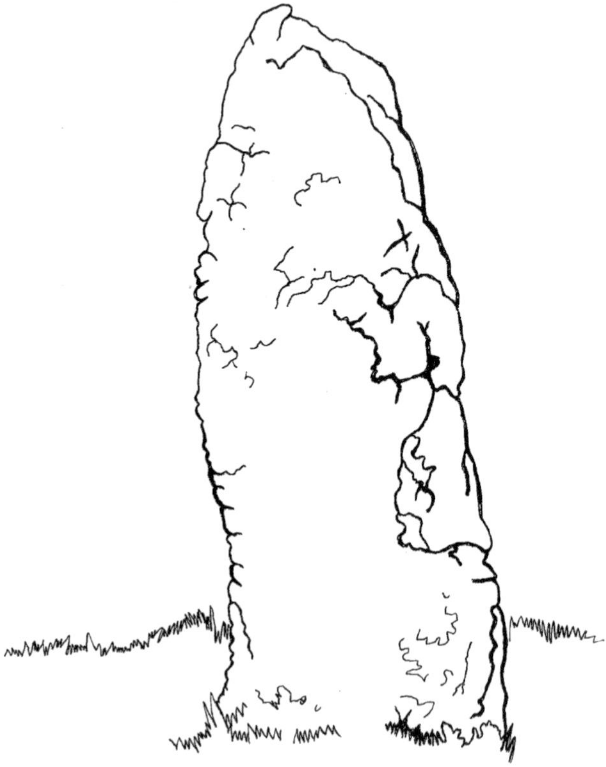

Le Manio, the menhir

release of emotion that came from goodness knew where, and up into my awareness.

New sorrows mingled with old: childhood nightmares, along with the prolapsed uterus of a frightened young woman; my father, in life and early death, waxy in his coffin. I saw my mother terrified, and her mother before her, a crippled body already wasting in a wooden wheelchair before she was thirty. Then I saw *her* mother, my great-grandmother, raped in a pogrom on another continent. Now I was the young woman in our tragic line; would I, unlike those women before me, make it through in one piece?

I wept for all my female forebears, then for myself. My whole family—first the women, then the men—came into view, each one so wounded, each one evoking so much pathos. I clung to the granite, my teeth clacking against it as I cried.

Not pathos, compassion.

"But they were so afraid!"

And you?

"Of course me, yes. I am flesh of their flesh, carrying their legacy of disaster within my bones. I could have been my mother, going mad, or my grandmother, crippled beyond repair. Why should I be any different?"

I shuddered against the stone, having no answer to my question. My tears had darkened the granite at the level of my face and I stared blearily at the mark. I felt the same helpless despair I knew so intimately from both my mother and grandmother, and I felt the energy drain right out through my feet. Defeated, my body slumped heavily against the stone, hiccoughing.

Change the family pattern by finding the natural pattern.

A fresh burst of tears came as I saw how circumstances—war, poverty, and ignorance—had derailed my people away from their birthright, generation after generation. I was the first in my line to have the luxury of even considering finding a natural pattern. I saw helpless despair being masked with bravado, and fear sliding into impotent rage. I saw my bloodline, the gene pool from which I came, coping as best they could with unthinkable oppression. I saw them fleeing the places they knew, resettling in a strange land, sick and ignorant and lost. I imagined myself in their place. Could I have survived?

You have.

"Not what they had to survive."

All the more reason to heal yourself, and, therefore, them. Find the natural pattern. Reinstate it.

I began to weep again and realized that, unlike them, I was not alone. I had these magic stones to guide and support me. Such extraordinary luck!

They did, too. They just did not know it.

The air was quiet for a moment, then the sense of a chuckle.

Everyone does. All you have to do is ask.

"But I never asked!"

You ask every day.

That stopped me for a moment, until I realized that, in fact, I never stopped praying.

Wash your hands.

Wash my hands? Did I get that correctly?

Find the source of water.

Puzzled, I gave the ancient stone a pat, blew my nose, and wandered into the adjacent woods looking for water. At first I saw nothing, but then, hidden in a thicket of brambles and vines, I noticed a tumble of rocks. After a bit of digging and pulling, the rocks revealed themselves to be the crumbling remains of a *fontaine*, a basin to catch the upwelling of an underground spring.

Such *fontaines* are found scattered all over the Breton countryside, and the water that seeps into them is always frigid. The water apparently comes up from deep below the water table, and it is ancient water. Holy water, it was said. This one was no exception and, when I cleared the debris and pine needles away from the basin, the water that ran clear into my hands was colder than ice. Shivering, I washed my stiff hands, splashing frigid water onto my face and arms and neck, and was rubbing it into my hair when I saw a flash of red.

No! No! Where was my bike? He must have found it. Without knowing it, I had managed to return to Kerlescan the back way. "Help!" I screamed silently.

You know what to do.

"I do not."

Stay with the fear. Face it.

Grabbing in one steadying breath, I asked in as loud a voice as I could,

"Do you know why this water is so cold?" I emerged from the woods onto the path, my heart pounding but my face a mask of calm, as if there was nothing out of the ordinary about running into a lonely cripple on a dark morning in an isolated pinewood with a storm threatening. I could barely breathe. My bike, about twenty feet away, leaned against the tree where I had left it. Cautiously, I inched my way toward it, never turning my back to him. I kept a friendly smile fixed on my face and chattered mindlessly about cold water and old *fontaines*.

"It is in the shade of the trees, of course," he replied. "In the dark." Keeping a wide berth between us, step by step, I made my way closer to my bike, always smiling while I kept up a steady babble about the coming storm and that I had better make my way home right away.

"Embrasse moi," he croaked. I shook my head hard. Compassion for him would come later, perhaps, but right now I just had to get out of there.

"I cannot, *Monsieur,*" I told him in as respectful voice as I could manage, adding in English, "I wish I could, really. I wish I weren't so afraid of you. I wish you weren't so needy, and I wish there was someone who truly loved you. But it cannot be me, even though I wish it could, because I'm not brave enough."

Not yet.

By that time I was safely at my bicycle, and throwing one leg over the seat I pushed down hard on the pedal, took off in a spurt of pine needles, and got out of the woods as fast as I could. I headed straight for town and my favorite *pâtisserie* shop, where I promised myself something flaky and creamy and chocolate, maybe more than one, and a café latte, hot enough to burn my tongue and warm my insides, until my heart settled down and my mind cleared enough that my hands wouldn't tremble.

Then I would sit at a table in the warm café and write in my journal everything I could remember about the lives of my mother and her mother, and of the Russian great-grandmother I had never met.

II. Kerfraval – afternoon, raining and cold

FORTIFIED WITH SUGAR, I was back home and tucked into a warm bed by the time the church bells of St. Cornély began ringing for Sunday Mass. Lying back on my pillow, I spent much of the rest of the dark day alternately dozing and reading about the history of the region. During the sixth and seventh centuries, I read, Christians were threatened with excommunication from the Church if they continued with their *adoration de pierres*, stone-worship, and, in A.D. 769, Charlemagne declared that those farmers who did not destroy all standing stones found in their fields would be excommunicated.

Vandalism of the stones, I read, continued as recently as the turn of the century, when the fanatical Abbé Jacques Corteaux of the Carnac region ordered the removal of scores of stones from the alignments to create a military base. Apparently, he piled them up to create an enormous altar on which were placed crucifixes, Christian statues, and plaques quoting his own poetry. Affixed to the pile was an explanatory plaque carved with the words: The Debris of a Bloody Cult.

I lay back wondering about evil, and how much a single madman was capable of perpetrating before the rest of us stopped him. Or her. Every generation, it seemed, produced evil geniuses who managed to determine the course of history. Hitler was one in our own time; the Abbé Corteaux, in his own self-righteous way, fifty years earlier, was another.

In the case of the megaliths, once upon a time tens of thousands of them around the world had been placed with purpose and skill for the benefit of the human community, using a technology we have since lost. They were wantonly destroyed in succeeding centuries for reasons we can only guess at: ignorance of their significance, greed, fear of their power? But why ? And what is their power?

Curled tightly around my pillow, my belly cramping, I fell fast asleep with my conundrum unresolved. When I awoke, the clouds were lifting and, ready for a comforting bowl of hot soup, I dressed to go out.

Madame Briard met me at the door: Monsieur Briard had hurt his back. Would I be willing to take a look at him?

I started to explain, again, that he would be better off going to the doctor, but then I thought better of it. I could take a quick look to make sure nothing was seriously injured, I told her, but then, if the family was willing, we would all go to

Kercado together for the healing. It was a good excuse to introduce the family to this amazing place they were fortunate to live so near.

In the end, not only did the whole family come but so did half the neighborhood, including the children. We went in two cars, one driven by the woman with the prolapsed uterus. I had to give directions because nobody else knew the way. At the site, the air had the fragrant, pristine quality of air after a good rain, and the pines dripped delicately onto the mulch of the forest floor. The children, having been cooped up indoors all day, immediately clambered onto the mound, chasing each other around the standing stone on top and tripping over its gorse and brambles.

"Why don't we do the healing inside the chamber?" I suggested, feeling a bit like a circus acrobat about to perform a daredevil stunt. The darkness inside would be spooky, no doubt about it, maybe muddy, too. The lot of us, crawling in on our knees, could well produce a bit of mayhem, but that made it more memorable for all of us. I reminded them that this was one of the most ancient known sites in all of Europe, and very sacred. They were duly impressed.

"I'll go in first with Monsieur Briard," I said.

He and I went in together, crouching. I spread my poncho on the damp ground, wrapping him up in a wool blanket. He lay down with much easing and groaning, while the others crawled in behind us. Monsieur Briard was clearly in pain, and for a moment I regretted that I had not kept things simpler and done the healing in the comfort of his own warm house. But everyone was excited, and all around us in the dark were hushed giggles and the cozy sound of many people breathing, preparing themselves for a ritual. We had somehow created sacred space together. I got a sense of how dolmens must once have been used, and was glad we had come.

Closing my eyes, I put my hands on his back. Nobody made a sound. I felt the bunched-up muscle right away, and it was a simple thing to knead it gently with my thumbs and the heels of my hands. Eventually the knot loosened, and he breathed a sigh of relief. I patted him to indicate that the healing was over and helped him to gingerly sit up. Everyone else was riveted.

"Pain's gone," he announced gruffly, rubbing the place where the pain had been, embarrassed to find himself sitting in the dark in the hills behind the town dump, surrounded by all his neighbors.

"I told you!" exclaimed Madame Briard, as everyone started talking about the miracle that had just occurred. I tried to explain that I had just massaged a sprained muscle, but nobody listened. By the time we had all left the chamber and were tromping back to the cars, my undeserved reputation was assured for all time.

III. Kercado – early morning, clear and mild

IN THE EARLY MORNING I went back to Kercado, alone this time. The sky, through the rainwashed trees, shone pink and yellow with the new day's sun, and crows cawed in the pine boughs. Except for some footprints in the mud in front of the chamber, there was little trace of the neighborhood crowd that had passed through here just twelve hours earlier.

"What do I do if people keep coming to me for healings?" I silently asked.

Relax.

I waited for more, but that was the only answer I received. I felt my body begin to subtly rock with my breathing, as it had done at the alignments. The tiny motions were elliptical, causing spirals and circles to appear and disappear behind my eyes until I was dizzy.

Relax.

Circles traced wider circles, then smaller ones; circles entwined with other circles, some fast, some slow. The spiraling lightshow behind my eyes grew to a riotous crescendo, slowed, then gradually faded. I took a deep breath and shook my head to clear it.

All energy cycles.

My body felt as if I was spinning inside, as if I could follow the blood and breath circulating throughout my system, then out into the air and water of the world's winds and oceans. I was part of all the Earth's systems, accompanying the planet through each rotation of the sun and moon, through seasons and years, generations and eons. The energies of the world cycled through me and with me without end. I felt dizzy and had to lower my head.

Each at its own pace. Each in its own span of time.

I went very still, listening. Hardly taking in breath, my body felt like an empty room cleared of furniture; its windows wide open to the air. Without effort my spine straightened, and the world's breath entered me like a gentle breeze in a clear space. Bliss.

You are in sacred space.

I sat in rapt stillness for I knew not how long, until my knees began to ache. I stretched out my legs, slowly opening my eyes to daylight. I was surprised to find myself in the pine grove, with the menhir atop the mound against my back. Standing right below me in the clearing, camera in hand, was a stocky blond man with a kindly face.

"*Pardon*," he said in accented French, "I did not wish to disturb you."

I nodded, still unable to speak.

"Do you live here?" he asked.

"Not at all," I replied, finding my voice. "I am from America. I am here to study the megaliths. And you?"

"I am from Norway," he told me, "and there I am a doctor." I told him that I was also interested in healing and was here to study the healing energies of the stones. He admitted he was also and looked at me expectantly. For one wild moment I considered telling him about my invisible guides, but then thought better of it and remarked more conservatively,

"I have been wondering how people can work together with the stones to evoke the healing energies of this place."

He gazed thoughtfully at the ground and shook his head. I realized that I might already be treading on ground too controversial for a medical doctor. He remained silent, so I tried a poetic approach. I suggested that energies might cycle and include both the animate and inanimate world. I suggested that the patterns of humans and the patterns of the natural world might reflect each other. And then I shut up.

"Interesting," he said finally. "Well, strange, but interesting," and with that he waved goodbye and disappeared into the trees. I sighed and tried to regain the calm equanimity of my state before he had arrived, but it was hard. I felt a familiar sense of failure. Even though I was married to a scientist, I still had not learned ways to communicate with those whose analytical minds perceived the world as composed of separate objects. This Norwegian doctor had got my back up, and my calm state was gone. Irritated, I stood and stomped down to where my backpack lay on the grass.

Suspend judgment. This came with a tone of gentle teasing, but I wasn't in the mood.

Later, as I was jotting notes in my journal, the doctor returned. He found me stretched out on the grass barefoot, writing in my notebook and munching on an apple.

"Hello again," he said quietly. For a moment I wondered if I should be afraid. "Um, you said you are interested in healing?" he asked hesitantly. I looked up, waiting for him to say more. "I have an injury in my hand that has never properly healed, and, well, as long as I'm here and you… " We each took a deep breath.

"I can only try," I admitted to him. "It will probably seem very strange to you, and of course I cannot guarantee an outcome. And I'm only a student of this process… " He cut me off in my litany of disclaimers.

"I am sincerely curious," he told me humbly.

"Well, then… "

I took him to the stone on top of the mound, and we stood on either side of it. Closing my eyes, I brought back the sense of sacred space I had felt here earlier and asked for help. It came immediately in the form of an impulse to place my hands on his left shoulder blade. His back was tight and I stayed there, feeling the crown of my head prickle and heat course through my hands into his body. In between his shoulder and shoulder blade I sensed a hard darkness, and my thumbs found the place and pressed gently. He sucked in a breath of pain, and I let up on the pressure. Holding one hand protectively over the spot, with the other I brushed downward on his left arm, as if pulling out the pain. Then I stroked his lower arm and wrist until I felt a release, and for a long while held his left palm in both of mine, gently drawing out what felt to me like stringy, prickling darkness.

"Shake out both arms," I whispered, my mind still focused on his shoulder. He shook them out, awkwardly at first, then more easily. "Breathe," I reminded him. He breathed. "Might you be willing to make some sounds?" I demonstrated by groaning softly, and sighing. Self-consciously, he joined in, and soon we were both coughing and growling and laughing at ourselves. This was certainly not medicine as he was accustomed to practicing it!

When we were quiet again there were tears brimming in his eyes, which were very blue. I felt the energy gradually simmer down, leaving me feeling replete and humbled. We stood quietly together for a few moments, then he motioned for us to sit while he told me his story.

In the war he had been shot in the shoulder. A piece of shrapnel was still in there, and indeed his hand problems dated from that time. How had I gone straight there, when his complaint had been about his hand?

"I don't know," I confessed. "I just follow my intuition, and my intuition led me to your shoulder. How long ago did this happen?" For the next hour we exchanged stories of our lives. He told me about his life near the fjords, and I told him about California and about living with a scientist and my ongoing frustration with all the presumptions inherent in the scientific mindset.

"All I want is for science to *listen* to other possibilities," I complained, and he nodded, vowing never to be sceptical about this kind of healing again. I grinned and told him he probably would be, as soon as he found himself in a room with other doctors.

"No, I will never forget this day," he declared, "and if you would not mind sitting up there against the stone as you were when I first saw you, I will take your photograph to make sure I do not."

"Thank you," he said quietly, as I settled in at the base of the stone, crossing my legs and closing my eyes, entering again the sweet stillness of meditation. In moments he was all but forgotten, and when I next opened my eyes he was gone. Later, when I got onto my bike and started back out on the trail, I realized I had never even asked his name, or told him mine.

6

Natasha

Quiberon

THE PULL OF THE STONES was constant, and there were times we felt comfortable only in their presence; yet, delighted as we were in their company, we also wanted to free ourselves for a few hours and be normal tourists as well. So, with that in mind, we drove inland from the Carnac alignments toward the town of Auray and paid a visit to the Quartier St-Goustan, which lies on the opposite bank of the river. It is an attractive and lively place, with many people enjoying the view of the river from the old and imposing stone bridge. There are little shops and restaurants, and several elegant cafés with brightly striped awnings over the tables outside. High up on a wall, a blue-painted statue of the local saint holds a fish half his size, while looking down on the town and the passersby. No doubt he is there to encourage the local fishermen, but we were reminded that the fish, in classical times, was also a reference to the goddess Aphrodite—or Venus. This became relevant again later in the day.

Glancing into the window of an antique shop, I saw a picture that took me by surprise. On an easel was an oil painting of a standing stone on a beach facing out to sea. Unable to resist I went into the shop, where I examined the painting in detail, again feeling the lure of the stones—it seemed we were not being allowed to take days off, after all. While I wasn't interested in buying the picture, I asked the proprietor if she knew where it had been painted. Somewhat bemused, she gave us directions to where that stone and others might be found on the Quiberon coast. After that, we could hardly wait to leave the bustling little town and make our way back toward Carnac and Quiberon.

The *Côte Sauvage* is the wilder side of the peninsula facing the sea, and there we did indeed find a number of standing stones, some knee deep on the sandy beach, others higher up on the cliffs. The distance between them made it unclear if they had once been part of an alignment or grouping, or what their relation-

St-Goustan with fish

ship to each other might have been. We would have to investigate further.

Quiberon is a long narrow projection into the Atlantic, some fifteen kilometers in length but a mere three kilometers wide at its broadest. Those standing stones would not have been sited on a beach originally, but inland, as the whole area surrounding the Gulf of Morbihan has long since been inundated by rising seas. Some stone circles, such as those on the island of Er Lannic, are now partly submerged, revealing themselves only at low tide.

We could not identify the stone in the painting with certainty, but that was immaterial, as it had served to guide us to the others. Deciding to stay the night in order to explore the region more carefully, we booked into a small hotel close to the beach, then set off on foot with map, camera, and dowsing rods in hand. Following a rough, sandy track with shady woodland on one side and a go-kart course on the other, we went in search of a menhir clearly shown on the map but not so easy to find on the ground. Then we saw it: a large standing stone, taller than any of those we had found closer to the shore, securely fenced in a grassy enclosure smaller than a room in a house.

Cooped up in this rather undignified way, but surrounded by shrubs and flowers, the old weathered stone lit by the last rays of the evening sun looked like a great head. A face emerged from the shadows, a face that was not quite human, with large slanted eyes looking downward above an elongated nose and wide upturned mouth, the features set over a long pointed chin. It was beautiful, like a Madonna by Modigliani. Even though we could not get close to it because of the fencing, in the light of the setting sun it radiated a warm welcome for us. The feeling was one of recognition, as if it had been waiting for our arrival, as if the other stones had informed it that we would be coming to pay our respects.

It seemed to tell me about itself then, and I learned that its face had been deliberately weathered by elemental entities, the beings of Fire, Air, and Water, into a shape—a face—symbolizing love for the Earth felt by extraplanetary beings, especially those from Venus.

That bright planet was apparently of great importance to the astronomer-priests of the megalithic era. Repeating its orbital pattern every eight years, it is observable many times in the span of a human life and provides for us a beautiful illustration of our relationship with Earth's nearest planet.

The Goulvars menhir, Quiberon

I asked the menhir its age and was told that it had stood there for 5,000 years. When I asked how many years before Christ—B.C.—it had stood there, I received no response. Telepathically, I explained that Jesus had been one of many teachers who showed people how to live in harmony with each other, but his message had become so distorted over time that humans often did not know what to believe. I also said that according to American Indian spiritual beliefs, Venus is the planet to which humans eventually go in spirit.

Our Venusian friend responded positively to this explanation. It said that this was so, and that it too was a living being, a living *mineral* being, and like humans, still evolving. Its location in this place had been arranged by beings who had once come to Earth from Venus. After settling in Mesopotamia, they had moved across our planet, positioning stones at significant points, some as markers of the energy lines, others to serve as portals, as gateways for astral travel in light-bodies. To some, these beings were known as the Shining Ones.

I was told, too, that beings from Venus, and others from the mineral kingdom and elemental realms had, in those earlier times, existed in natural harmony with each other and the Earth, having little need of teachers. The voice acknowledged, however, that now humans *do* have such a need. We seem to have lost our once-universal ease with harmonious existence, a loss that has triggered numerous catastrophes not only for humanity but for the natural world as well.

This particular stone had once been the marker of such a portal to other realms, which had long since gone out of use. It apparently had no wish to be reactivated until such time as the surrounding area was also energetically reactivated. This would only be possible with the conscious interaction of large numbers of people. The fact of our recognition and respect—Hamilton's and mine—was apparently not enough. There had to be a more general awareness of the natural life force of the land before restoration could be truly effective.

The stone continued to tell its story. Many people, it said, were only now becoming aware that the Earth upon which they live and have their being is a conscious, living being itself rather than an inert lump of rock. I was reminded of the book, *Gaia*, in which author James Lovelock writes about the Earth as a conscious being, in relationship with all its inhabitants, including us humans, and how shocking Lovelock's ideas were to many people when the book first came out.

There are other stones, I learned—even some of those right there on the beach—that had also been intended as portals for travelers in their light-bodies, but none were presently in use. The spiritual energy of today is of insufficient vitality to sustain such travelers. At this, a shadow passed over our stone friend and, for an instant, its loving face wore a serious expression.

You have work to do, I heard.

The following day we visited all the other menhirs we could find in the area. They seemed purposefully silent in their random placements, facing each other or looking inscrutably out to sea from the beaches and rocky headlands of a spiritually impoverished landscape. Now we had been told why they were asleep and what would eventually awaken them—there was no need to add anything further. The moment for their reawakening had not yet come, for much work elsewhere still needed to be done.

As we said farewell to our new friends, we promised to return when the time was right.

Locmariaquer

LOCMARIAQUER, THE PLACE OF MARY, is an attractive fishing village of Roman origin clustered around an old church, a few miles from the island of Gavrinis in the Gulf of Morbihan. Facing the church is a small hotel. We had a pleasant rest there, after a walk on the white sandy beach, which was scattered with young families on holiday.

Archaeology has uncovered traces of the first settlement to be built here 6,000 years ago. The many remaining megaliths bear witness to the rituals of the neolithic people who once lived in the area. A place where the sacred energies of Earth and Heaven meet, Locmariaquer was clearly a significant location and most likely played an important role in the prehistoric Carnac complex.

There are several impressive dolmens, including the well-known restored group of La Table des Marchand and the huge, closed burial tumulus of Er-Grah, but the most famous stone of all is Le Grand Menhir Brisé, a three-hundred-ton colossus, which lies beside them, broken into four pieces. This single menhir, which once stood more than sixty feet tall, is one of the largest known examples, exceeded only by the one-hundred-foot-high stele, or inscribed monument stone, at Aksum in Ethiopia.

Made of finely shaped granite of a type not found in the locality, it is hard to understand how, so long ago, it could have been transported and erected on this spot. Traditionally called the Faery Stone by the local people, it was originally the terminus of a row of eighteen great monoliths that grew in height from north to south. At one moment in history, it is thought that changing beliefs resulted in the biggest one being deliberately split apart with wooden wedges and felled, no mean achievement for the time. The top section evidently broke as it hit the ground, and the four pieces have lain there ever since.

The other stones in the row were dismantled as well. Some were reused to cover the dolmen chambers that were then built on nearby sites, replacing earlier timber structures. The postholes of these structures have been uncovered. Archaeologists identified three fragments of what had once been a single menhir, an impressive forty feet high, as coming from the same standing stone when they discovered that the lines of cleavage and engraved images of large-horned oxen and a plough matched up. One section now covers the burial chamber of the Er-Grah tumulus, and another seventeen-ton piece forms the roof-slab of the remarkable Gavrinis cairn and only revealed the carved images on its upper face during the reconstruction a few years back.

The third section of that stone was reused also, serving as the covering of La Table des Marchand during its construction, probably around 5,500 years ago. At that time, the large backstone of the inner chamber, already set in the ground as a single stele, was incorporated into the new structure. It is carved in relief on both sides. The face now visible has a design of multiple "shepherd's crooks" arranged in four rows, perhaps symbols of the vital energy held in the solar, or ley line, upon which it stands. Even today it holds power, and although normally quiescent, it can still surprise an unwary tourist by giving off an electric shock. A replica now replaces that stone, no doubt once guarded night and day by a vigilant priesthood, and the original is preserved in the Carnac museum. The uprights that form the sides of the entry passage also came originally from yet another recycled menhir.

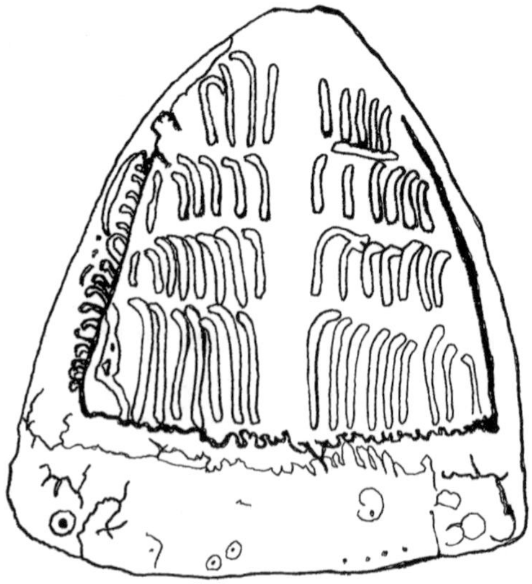

Backstone from La Table des Marchand

In time, what may have originally been a temple became a place of burial for the bones and small treasures of revered ancestors. Facing the winter solstice sunrise, it marks the time of renewal of the light, enabling the departing spirit to break away from earthly ties and move on to another sphere.

The ley line that can be dowsed there acts as a link between La Table des Marchand and the original position of the great broken menhir. At that point it intersects another straight energy line, which itself connects with the fine standing stone known as Le Manio, near the alignments in Carnac. Le Manio inspired Carolyn when she was there, and the two of us many years later, providing information for our previous book, *Let The Standing Stones Speak.*

There were many tourists at Locmariaquer when we were there, indicating to us that more people are feeling a resonance with these megalithic sites and probably wondering, as we do, what motivation might have led those people of long ago to put so much work and dedication into the moving, and setting in place, of such massive stones. It was encouraging to find the place well visited, but the proximity of so many people made it a little difficult for us to "tune in."

Usually, we have found ourselves alone and undisturbed at the stones, but lately, with more distractions around us, we have had to learn how to concentrate to receive information about the energies of these numinous relics of our past. This time it came visually, as images in the mind, as if I were watching a hazy film.

In ancient times, during significant annual solar events, the local community could ritually attune with the terrestrial currents of energy at this site, and in my mind's eye, I saw the traces of long-gone people dancing up and down, weaving between and around the columns of stone in serpentine lines. Such formal activity—dancing in slow hypnotic patterns—has often been part of ancient rituals. It acts as a trigger to connect the physical forces in the human body with those of the spiritual Cosmos, activating and releasing energy at all levels. As the terrestrial spiral was raised higher through each column of stone, it would connect with a cosmic spiral drawn down, a meeting of the earth serpent with the cosmic serpent in a two-way flow of activity; a double helix of positive and negative energy in perfect balance, like the Caduceus symbol. Thus, a powerful feeling of unity, of "belonging" to the environment, was readily experienced by people, as the flow passed along the solar lines, revitalizing them and their surroundings and expanding outward across the landscape.

Such ceremonies would have been held at the solstices and equinoxes, and also at particular phases of the moon, when it reflected the paler light of the sun back onto Earth. Human participation in the natural ebb and flow of energy at significant times of the year is essential for a wholesome relationship with the Earth and with its cycles, in order that community life continue in health and harmony. That is a practice once built into our lives that we have forgotten, to our great loss.

The spiraling of energy through these stones had been intensified by that earlier human participation. And it seemed to me that every standing stone, once so carefully placed, had the function of marking the veiled but discernible lines of energy for each group of local people. As in church spires and Muslim minarets, they drew down the planetary energies and transformed them for the benefit of Earth and all its myriad forms of life.

Such spirals of energy around the great menhirs perhaps existed before the placement of the stones. They are perceptible even now by dowsing, even though the stones have long since gone. But the connection and potential of communion with the cosmic forces there, so fundamental to human evolution, would have been broken by the removal of the stones. Something was lost that could be brought back only by replacing them, then only with the conscious intention that must have existed in earlier times. I was sadly reminded of the bleak Quiberon landscape, where we had found so many inactive stones.

In neolithic times, the Earth would have had a much greater "soul energy" than can presently be experienced, a subject that was the focus of the extensive writings of the philosopher and teacher Rudolf Steiner. For thousands of years, human souls understood themselves to be integral parts of their environment, experiencing intuitively their deep connection with the forces that activate the Cosmos and are radiated to Earth. In fact, it was the megalithic era that signaled the end of such sensitivity. The erection of standing stones all over the planet during that extended period was a dramatic action, initiated by astronomer-priests, to "hold the force" that our ancestors were starting to lose, and to keep it marked until it could be restored and worked with once again.

In my mind's eye, I saw those first astronomer-priests. More of the spirit world than the physical world, they taught mankind about the Earth's relationship with the rest of the solar system. Eventually they had to leave the planet when it began to lose the spiritual animation they required to sustain themselves. As in the Irish folktales, they seem to have retreated into their temple mounds, dematerializing back to another dimension. Might they, like Merlin, reappear when needed?

After the loss of guidance by the astronomer-priests, our ancestors found it hard to continue the appropriate ritual observances on their own. As the atmosphere of Earth increased in density, so did the lower forces of negative emotions. It was then that a new kind of priest took over, concerned less with sharing spiritual experience than with personal power and the exercise of control over others. A sense of fear and separation in people steadily increased in the era of organized religions that followed, ushering in the material and competitive society in which we still live.

The removal and destruction of the great stones took place along with the loss of faith in the old ways. Nevertheless, some who ranked as leaders during the age that followed retained aspects of the old knowledge inherited by the priesthood of ancient civilizations in Egypt, Central America, and Mesopotamia; for instance, the levitation of massive stones. Modern experiments have shown that the heaviest stone people can readily move, using oak rollers and levers, is a thirty-two-ton block on the level, but since we know that blocks of stone of three hundred tons and more were once moved and lifted, we wonder if some ancient technology might have been used that rendered stone weightless by temporarily suspending the force of gravity? How might it have been done at Baalbek, for example, at Machu Picchu, or in the Sphinx Temple and the Giza Pyramids? Whatever these people knew is no longer understood in our contemporary world, which may be just as well as it would no doubt be misused.

Knowledge we do retain today, however, in a mainly scientific context, is the power of the three-dimensional spiral. We know that it is inherent in both our environment and our consciousness, from the double helix of physical DNA, to the weather patterns of our earthly atmosphere, to the spiral forms of the galaxies. It is found in Nature in the whirling of water, in seashells and snails, in the spiraling growth of leaves on plants, in the helical structure of sunflower seedheads and pinecones—in fact, just about everywhere we look in the natural world.

Geometrically, the same progressive harmonic patterns of Nature are demonstrated in the Fibonacci number series, which produces an ever-expanding and elegant spiral into infinity. In mathematical terms, each number in an ascending scale

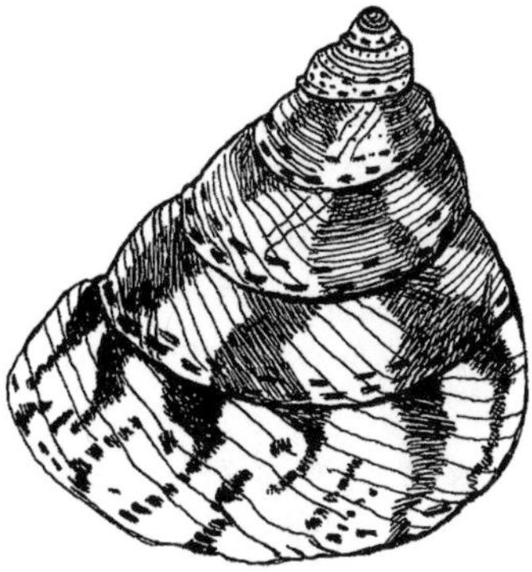

Spiral seashell

is the sum of the two preceding it, and the ratio of each to the next gets closer and closer to the perfect proportion of the Golden Mean, yet never quite achieves it—perhaps a parallel to all human endeavor. It is recognized in Islam that human art forms should embody imperfections, reflecting the belief that only the Creator is perfect. In Islamic calligraphy and architectural design, there is always some small detail built in that doesn't quite match the rest. That may also be symbolic of the random, chaotic element in Nature that leads, over time, to changes in structure and form.

One of my own experiences of the invisible spiral of energy took place in Normandy, on a hilltop Celtic site. Hamilton and I had been urged to visit the site by a friend who felt we would enjoy the place, as he had. At first it appeared to be just a mass of earth and stone, the ruins of what had once been a thriving center; now deserted, it had been taken over by the Nature spirits once so revered by the Celtic peoples. We could feel them there, energetically in the ruins with us, as the place was so abundantly alive and green, trees and bushes sprouting out of every possible crevice of those huge mounds of stone.

We asked the invisible but almost tangible guardians for permission to enter and felt the place becoming more and more magical the farther into the woods we went. We were even afraid of getting lost in this wild place. I asked the *genius loci*, its guardian, to reveal some of its secrets to us, realizing that the Druid priests would certainly have chosen this site deliberately, being aware of some inherent quality in its energies. I wanted to know what that might be.

Attuning myself for a few moments, I turned to walk along a high stone ridge through the tangled trees, stopping where it opened up, free of undergrowth. The trees had not yet shed their leaves; there was plenty of green cover—shades of red and orange mingled with the yellowy-green of autumn. Quite suddenly, the view ahead became blurred and seemed to be flowing fast, like water. In between the blurry patches, I perceived bands of extreme clarity that, in contrast, were so sharply focused that the detailed veins of each leaf were visible.

Whatever was happening? As I stood very still and looked slowly around, to my amazement I saw that a huge spiral of moving energy surrounded me. I was at its center and was, indeed, being shown something of the hidden secrets of the place. How long it lasted I do not know because I had lost all sense of time. I seemed to have entered "timelessness," a peaceful yet powerful experience of being "at one" with everything. Later, I was grateful for this swirling, coiled vision of Earth energy, which slowly returned to normal appearance. When I recalled what I had experienced, I realized it was only when I had begun to analyze what I was seeing that the vision had faded away.

Spiral carving, Newgrange

We descended the hill and, looking at a diagram posted by the entrance, tried to locate where I had been standing in the spiral. It appeared to be over a former entrance, a gateway into the communal center. Perhaps this gateway once could radiate a protective beam of blessing on all who entered or left, like the spiral beam of energy often felt in a church, over the old baptismal font in its original setting upon an Earth spiral. Children baptized in those places received a bit of that magic, a blessing from the energy spiral itself, from the spirit of the Universe more than the spirit of religion. These children would have been dipped in the unpolluted water of life; the intent of the priest intoning prayers for their wellbeing and acceptance into the community would have activated the spiral.

Certain places on Earth, sited on the etheric pathways along which energy travels, are especially receptive to prayer and can activate healing and blessing. They are connected to other dimensions by spiral energies that are not normally seen, but can be felt or dowsed; these energies invariably respond to human stimulation by expanding when people practice healing, prayer, or blessing, meditation, dance, or music.

There are many accounts of miraculous healings taking place after people prayed beside images of saints of their particular religion, whose images were once deliberately placed at the site of a healing spiral. In our own experience, we have also found that these energetic vortices can be created, over time, by repeated devotional and healing practices. The force of an inspired vitality can then become attached to that place and will remain there.

Experienced dowsers are now discovering, and even measuring, these vortices at many places in the world: at the center of the Angkor Wat temple complex in

Unicursal labyrinth

Cambodia, for example; at standing stones in Japan; in New Zealand, at the Maori people's sacred sites. Certainly, these places of power, where energy spirals up from the Earth, were recognized everywhere by our own ancestors. They carved spiral symbols in the megalithic temples of Malta and on the megaliths of England and Scotland, Russia, France, and Germany, and upon the stones of the great ceremonial mounds of Newgrange and Knowth in Ireland.

The whirling dervish dance of the Sufis, spinning first one way, then the other, demonstrates perfect spiritual balance in the spiral. Young children everywhere do this, too, turning round and round in circles just like whirling dervishes, and when they fall over they can still feel that magical spinning energy. Finally, the spiral form is seen in the unicursal, or one-way labyrinth, where the path continuously turns back upon itself into the center, causing those who walk it to experience a similar balancing energy to that of the whirling dervishes. Dowsing such a labyrinth after it has been walked shows that its invisible ring of energy expands in response to that human activity. The more human interaction it receives, the larger its energetic blueprint.

Once, labyrinths were numerous in the world, although only a few examples remain today. Some can still be seen in medieval churches in Western Europe—the one at Chartres, in France, being by far the most famous; others exist, cut into turf in the British Isles at the so-called Troytown Mazes or outlined in stone upon the Scandinavian seashore.

From its ancestral roots, the labyrinth has become a symbol for the spiritual journey of the human soul, a mode of meditating upon life itself.

7

Carolyn's Journal

I. Locmariaquer – noon, clear and hot

A NOISY MOTORBIKE spewing diesel fumes was vrooming up and down the rows when I arrived at Le Ménec. In a nearby field, a tractor rumbled to and fro, and on the road passing cars added to the din. Somewhere in the environs, I could even hear the high-pitched whine of a chainsaw. I couldn't bear the noise. Even in the best of times, I was sensitive to machine noise but now, in my hyper-receptive state, it was more than I could tolerate. At times like this, I wondered if I were made to live in the modern world.

You have no choice.

"But it makes me crazy!"

Don't worry, it will get worse.

"I am not in the mood for humor!"

Take the path of least resistance.

"But how?"

Leave.

"Oh." The obvious had not occurred to me.

Go. There is no time to waste.

I stood up, stashed my notebook in my backpack, and strode away from Le Ménec toward the road, nearly bumping into a tall young man on the path who reminded me of my younger brother. I smiled automatically, holding out my hand. His name was Dédé, and he came from Besançon, he told me. He was on vacation before school started again in the fall. We chatted easily, as fellow tourists do, and I complained about the volume of local noise.

"I'm getting out of here before it makes me crazy," I told him.

"Have you been to Locmariaquer?" he asked. Locmariaquer, several kilometers away, was a place Jiri and I had avoided because it drew so many tourists, but its standing stone was said to be the largest in the world, more than sixty feet tall.

Le Grand Menhir Brisé

Now it lay in four massive, broken pieces on the ground and, while archaeologists have said it was deliberately toppled, nobody really knew. I had hoped to get there before I left Brittany.

"No, I haven't been there yet, and yes, I would love to go," I laughed, sassily assuming I had been invited. He laughed with me, and in moments we planned our getaway.

The timing of this synchronicity was perfect.

See how it works? When you feel the impulse, trust it and follow it!

I grinned at the cunning of the lesson and Dédé, assuming the smile was for him, grinned back. We hid my bike in the bushes, walked to his car, and he held open the door for me. It never occurred to me to worry that I was getting into a car with a man I had only just met. The coincidence of our meeting at that precise moment made it completely safe. It was so simple: I was exactly where I wished to be, on my way to see the Broken Menhir of Locmariaquer with a nice young man with brown eyes whom I had known for less than ten minutes. Silently, I thanked my guides.

Even on the ground, in four helter-skelter pieces, the Grand Menhir Brisé was larger than anything I could have imagined. It was at least twice the size of Le Manio and, standing alongside even the smallest of the pieces, Dédé and I were dwarfed. We read in the guidebook that there had once also been here a long barrow with chambers, perhaps used for burials, and that the stone was carved from quartzite granite mined many miles away.

How in the world had people transported three hundred tons of a single piece of granite all that distance, long before the wheel had been invented? Why had it been important enough to do so? Who were these people for whom we had no history—only an extraordinary array of standing stones marching all over this seaside landscape?

My guidebook claimed that the various stone sites in the Carnac region all formed part of an astronomical complex—the alignments being refined instruments capable of foretelling eclipses—and that this huge menhir was the center of a vast lunar laboratory spread across the Breton landscape. I recalled the cider lady's slap of her thigh, exclaiming, "That's another one!" and figured she probably had done the same thing with the fellows who had told her *that* one when they had stopped in for a drink.

Who could say that the stones were *not* an astronomical observatory? Who could say that they were not *also* an astronomical observatory? Who could say the information coming to me from goodness knew where was any less valid? It could, of course, be that I had an overactive imagination, but that didn't explain how someone like Jiri, a cool-headed scientist, could receive information as well as I could.

Shhh. Settle.

I felt an impulse toward a large dolmen across the meadow and followed it, leaving Dédé with a group of tourists and their guide. At the dolmen, I ducked in and crept into its dark depths, settling down against granite. Immediately, patterns of circles began to appear again, like the colorful designs in a kaleidoscope.

Bursting lines of light spun behind my eyes, psychedelic wheels with hubs like standing stones. The wheels shimmered and merged, an ever-expanding mandala stunning in its intricacy and also in its utter simplicity. The design had no beginning and no end, only infinite connection to everything, everywhere.

Everything is connected to everything.

How could I not trust this voice?

Links in a chain of being.

"Is that what these stoneworks are all about?"

Partly.

Then I got a vision of blood circulating in my body and saw that it carried everything—nutrients, oxygen, energy—to all my organs, limbs, skeleton, brain. When the flow got stuck, I got sick. It had to be the same for the Earth.

Macrocosm and microcosm are the same.

Of course.

Everyone can restore the balance.

How? When I had sung at the edge of the sea with Jiri, I had known in my bones something of what I was being shown right now. I could still feel the glorious perfection of that song, the rapture of that effortless singing, the love I had felt for Jiri.

You were attuning.

Attuning, yes, that's right! Literally and figuratively. It had been the most fun time of our whole week together, and our music had been utterly beautiful. We were completely in synch with each other and the world.

Pleasure is the key, of course.

So simple, so obvious. How could this essential wisdom have ever been forgotten, and how do we get it back?

Love.

That's all?

Learn how to love.

For a long time I sat in thrall, awed by what I had just received. The truth of it percolated through my body and mind, settling like a vow in my whole being.

Learn how to love. I waited to hear more, but all I received was the merest sense of a pat on the head, as if to say it was no big deal, and that it was also the whole thing, and that it was time to go meet up with my new friend again.

I left the dolmen feeling lightheaded, dancing a little two-step. When I found Dédé, I wrapped my arms about his neck. He blushed happily and suggested we go out for lunch, which we did, dining upon crêpes and oysters in an outdoor café at the edge of the sea, with sun and salt wind in our faces and good conversation about all matter of things. After this day we would most likely never meet again, but for right now we were kin, connected to each other by all the invisible threads that had made us cross paths in the first place. For one day, we had roamed a small bit of the world together, having a good time, sharing some thoughts, and delighting in knowing each other.

That is love.

It's not more complicated than that?

Easy as pie. Sticky as molasses.

I laughed out loud. "It's *you* I'm in love with, my invisible friend, whoever and wherever you are!"

Later that day, returning hand in hand to Le Ménec to retrieve my bike, Dédé and I found that the tires were flat as a pancake, the air having been mischievously let out, probably by local kids playing a prank. Gentleman that he was, Dédé roped my useless bike to the roof of his car and drove me home. I hung out the window to steady the bike as it lurched and clanged there on the roof, and we laughed every inch of the way—and then some.

II. Tumulus St-Michel – afternoon, fogbound

FROM THE TOP OF THE TUMULUS the sea was lost in a layer of fog, and the alignments, spread out below, were barely visible beneath a low-lying mist. The air swirled wet about me, and the stones below seemed to appear and disappear, as if they were dancing in lines across the landscape, bobbing up and down, in and out. I watched in a kind of trance, following the undulating lines, and hearing—in my mind's ear—the beating of drums and the sound of many feet stamping the ground.

Watch.

I sat up straight, crossed my legs under me, and slipped into the state of calm attention that seemed to bring the teachings through most clearly. As if I were flying over the countryside, I saw all the stones—alignments, dolmens, the broken menhir, *everything*—as a single instrument, like one huge temple. There appeared to be gatherings of people fanning out through the alignments, dancing. I was shown a ceremony of healing and reconnection; of attunement with each other and the Earth and Heavens; of initiations into adulthood; of worship at phases of the sun and moon; of dancing and singing and praying and making love. It was all there in my vision, as these early people came together to reaffirm the sacredness of existence, and in so doing, to maintain the world.

Keep going bigger.

To maintain the whole Universe by being its microcosm! In my mind's eye, I saw Brittany itself stretch out toward other parts of the globe, until the stones at Carnac were only one point of a worldwide web. Oh!

Imagine the human body. Every limb, every organ, every cell is part of the whole. Watch.

Then, below me in the rows, I saw people—men and women, babies and elders—their bodies clothed in skins and feathers, with anklets of shells, and rattles in their fists. Some beat at drums in the stone circles, while others moved between the stones, chanting as they danced hypnotically to the beat, their shells rattling in close rhythm with the drums.

A Carnac alignment

Chants rose from the stone circles as the lines broke up and reformed, and when the dancers' beat grew ragged, a furious rattling brought them back into step. I watched, mesmerized, as I felt the members of the tribe come into balance with each other, the Earth itself pounding with the rhythm of their footfalls. I felt the energies latent in the stones become activated by the ritual dance of the people and sensed, in my blood, a restoration of natural order as earth realigned with heaven, and the people realigned with both.

Healing. Wholeness. Holiness.

As the dancers stamped up and down the stone rows, beat after beat, I could feel myself make subtle adjustments in my own body until I, too, was part of the dance. I was in harmony along with them. All I had to do was breathe and listen until some internal jangle, just barely in my awareness, smoothed out to a clear sound. I found myself crying then, as I seemed to be swept up in their ritual, invited to participate as one of them. My people. My Earth.

La participation mystique.

I was ecstatic. An old doubt was settled for me once and for all, as drums and dancers faded: I knew that I belonged to their tribe, no matter who they were or in what era they had danced. I was part of the world and always would be. Even if my unlikely experiences in Carnac were nothing but self-perpetuated fantasy, I knew now that I was part of a much vaster life than I had thought, and that it was beautiful.

In two days' time I would catch the train for Paris, and in three days I would be home. Tonight I would phone Jiri and tomorrow make my last visit to Kercado, but then my sights would be turned toward home and ordinary life as a wife and mother in the city. Who would believe me when I told them of my adventures? Would I even tell anybody?

I got up, shook the moisture off my poncho and, for the last time, descended the tumulus to where my bike was stashed in the broom bushes. I would go into

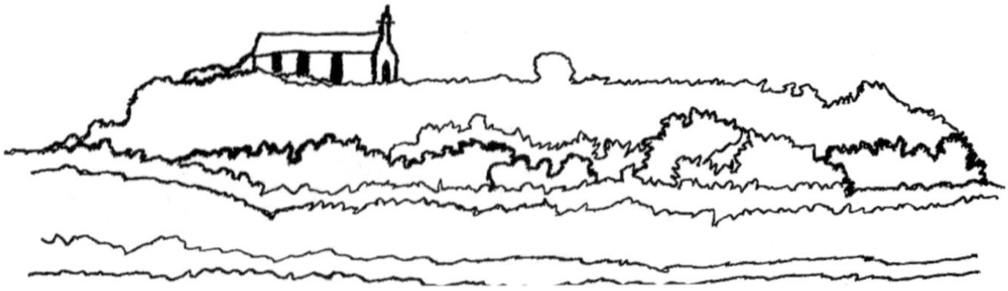

The tumulus and chapel

town for my last double latte and buy my favorite *pâtisseries,* saving one to eat tomorrow at Kercado, and sharing the others with the Briard family at our farewell dinner together tonight.

III. Kercado – last morning, bright

I AWOKE FROM A DREAM. In it, I am at the outdoor market in Carnac, buying French cheeses to bring home to my family. I notice that everyone in the market appears watchful, walking nervously and stopping often. I stand aside, looking around to see what is making them uneasy, and catch a glimpse of a lion's tawny pelt moving out of sight in the crowd. Like the others, I stop dead in my tracks, not breathing. The lion is out of sight, but just over there, by the vegetable stall, I think I hear the faint sounds of raspy breathing, followed by the flash of a yellow tufted tail disappearing into the crowd. Lions are in the marketplace, and we are their prey.

Melting into the background, I try to make myself invisible to them, keeping them visible to me. How to do that? I sniff the air for clues, catching a faint whiff of acrid lion breath, then another glimpse of tawny fur out of the corner of my eye. The glint of the lion's eye appears from behind the cheeses, and I hear the faint *pad pad* of velvet paws stalking slowly. I realize that my life depends upon my ability to intuit, by subtle perception, every "lion-ish" clue in the air. I must be absolutely still, observe with perfect attention, and sense subtle signals. I must hone the skill of every one of my senses, so that I am a master of awareness. I must know lions as well as if I were a lion myself, or I could be killed.

It was that simple.

I lay in bed for a long while, memorizing this dream of my last morning in Carnac, and then meditated while the sun climbed higher in the sky. Later on, having indeed gone to the outdoor market to buy French cheese to bring home to my family—and not seen any lions, of course—I cycled up the hill to Kercado for my last visit.

Entering the pinewood, I was touched to find the white cat sprawled in a shaft of sunlight atop the mound, as if she were waiting for me. I knelt by her side, stroking her silky fur while she purred contentedly, gazing at me with slit eyes.

"Has it been you all along?" I murmured, imagining her as my animal familiar, like in so many fairy-tales. "Are you the one who's been communicating with me?" I lifted her onto my lap and she offered no resistance. Then I bent over her, thanking whoever or whatever had taken such good care of me these past three weeks, and I kissed the top of her head. "I'll be back," I whispered in her ear.

No.

Clear as a bell, there was the voice.

Do not return. You belong in America.

"But… "

France is the old place. There is no time to waste. Go home.

"But, the stones are here."

Stones are everywhere, and we are everywhere. You have everything you need to continue. Go home!

For another twenty minutes I sat against my stone atop the mound, waiting for more, but it never came. The air was still, my mind empty. Finally, the white cat stretched and stalked away down the mound, disappearing into the shadows of the pinewood. She never looked back. It was time for me to do the same. Looking around Kercado for one last time, I stood pressed against my stone for a moment, and left.

8

Natasha

Kercado

ALONG WITH RECEIVING MESSAGES from certain stones, we have become aware that other sites in the region, long dormant, now seem to be slowly awakening. We are witnessing a revival of activity at this extraordinary and strange place, a conscious renewal of its original function as part of the Earth's energetic network.

An inner voice told me that the Kercado dolmen, one of the oldest in Europe and today ensconced in the wooded grounds of a château, had been dormant for more than four centuries. Like the princess waiting to be awoken by the prince's kiss in *Sleeping Beauty*, it had fallen asleep and been neglected during a general dimming of consciousness, as the world lost any ongoing, positive interaction between humans and the primal energies that permeate our planet. Perhaps it closed down at the time of the Inquisition, when both wise women and standing stones were feared by a patriarchal society and the Church did its best to suppress the old pagan practices.

This may be why many of us are drawn to the megaliths now and even feel at home with them. We recognize that our purpose is to reawaken and reactivate their energies, to enable the power of a higher consciousness to flow more freely through the Earth's meridians.

On one of our visits to Kercado, we arranged to meet a French couple who had contacted us after reading our book and who shared with us a deep connection to Carnac. Indeed, Nicole had moved from Paris to Brittany to be near the stones, where she felt "at home," while Alain had formerly been the official guardian of Kercado and knew it well. Both are active in the local conservation society.

Early in May 2006, Hamilton and I came to Kercado to meet them. Before they arrived, we spent time re-exploring the dolmen and were saddened to find that it seemed more neglected than before. It was damp inside the small chamber. The puddles of water on the floor made it difficult for us to keep our feet dry, so we

Kerzerho, a large stone

went and sat for a while at the standing stone on top of the mound, then stood by the lower stone opposite the entrance. Everything felt very quiet, as if it, too, were waiting.

We had just enjoyed an open-air lunch of buckwheat pancakes at a nearby *crêperie* that had not been there during Carolyn's visit, when Nicole and Alain came walking down the path. Although we had never met before, we recognized each other immediately; just as with the stones, we already felt like old friends. They brought dowsing rods, pendulum, and maps and told us about their research and experiences at Kercado, showing us a plan they had made of the connections between this site and others across the region.

The plan incorporated some of the findings of Scottish professor and engineer Alexander Thom, who surveyed and drew the definitive plans of so many of the stone circles of Britain and France. For example, just north of the eastern end of the Kermario row, Thom found a menhir marking a tumulus at the location was once visible from Le Géant du Manio, the tallest standing stone in the Morbihan area.

Le Géant is on the highest ground, and the alignment of the two may have indicated a particular sunrise in the celebratory cycle of the year. Other pairs of stones, pointing to the position on the horizon of extreme lunar risings and settings, would have been visible as similar markers for miles around, until their purpose was obscured by the more recent growth of trees.

We discovered later that the enigmatic stone marker of the tumulus has serpent engravings upon it below the ground level, which were only visible after it was re-erected some years ago. Since then, other stones have been found with similar snakelike carvings below ground level, an intentional and intimate connection with the vitality of the Earth. Naturally, like Le Géant, this menhir stands upon a dowsable energy line.

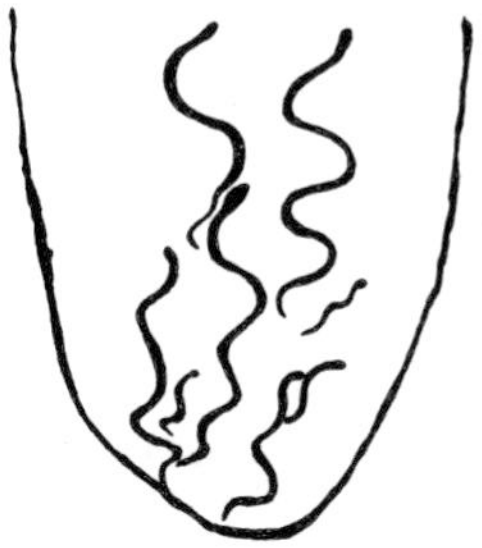

Snake carvings, Kermario menhir

Nicole and Alain mentioned finding large pulsating rings of energy around most single menhirs; such rings, often seven of them, can be dowsed inside a stone circle, as well as the encircling energy that alternates in polarity from each stone to the next. Sometimes, they said, dowsing will reveal etheric petal shapes around a standing stone, a pattern of eight petals corresponding to the four cardinal points, that may have been used to indicate the timing of the traditional solar festivals.

After a lively exchange of information, Nicole spoke of other, more mysterious things she had learned from the stones, particularly from the menhir that tops the Kercado mound. Once the word *Schumann* had come to her, which she assumed had to do with the composer. After reading our book, however, she realized that she was being reminded of the *Schumann Wave,* a low-frequency vibration that constantly pulses over the Earth's surface at an optimum frequency of just under 8 Hertz, or cycles per second. That frequency equates to the Alpha or relaxed rhythm of the human brain, thus allowing us to be comfortably in tune with our planet. There is also a musical connection, as at times she has heard at this place the eight musical notes that make up an octave.

We then went together into the dolmen, crouching low in the passageway, and entered the chamber, where we perched uncomfortably around the edge of the puddles. There is an electric light inside the chamber now, but it did not illuminate the dark space very well, so Alain used his torch to light up small symbols on the capstone that he had spotted when meditating there one dawn.

It was too dark and shadowed for us to make them out clearly, but the guidebook describes one as a badge shape, possibly a stylized goddess or earth mother, reflecting a time when men and women accepted equal responsibilities in the family and tribal group. The other is an axe with a handle, a stone tool of great importance, both practical and ritual, for all megalithic people.

The pottery, stone axes, flint arrowheads, pendants, and other objects recovered during several excavations of the dolmen show that it was in use from the neolithic period, beginning almost 7,000 years ago, through the Bronze Age, and even reused in the Iron Age—a very long history. The idea of a dolmen as a symbolic womb has often been noted, a place of rebirth for those whose bones were deposited there; why else would their useful and treasured possessions have also been interred there, if not for use in the afterworld?

Returning to the outside, we investigated the remains of the outer ring of stones that encircles the tumulus. The outer ring was once an integral part of the mound but is now considerably worn away by the passage of time. Most of its stones have gone missing, and some have fallen. As an energy center, Kercado definitely felt sluggish to us now and that a conscious input of energy would be needed to help restore its power. Positioning ourselves where the missing stones would have been, and asking for the cooperation of the Angelic realms to restore the life force there, we gradually began to feel lighter and eventually joyous as, laughing, we moved slowly around the circle, feeling a return of the natural flow of energy. The sense of

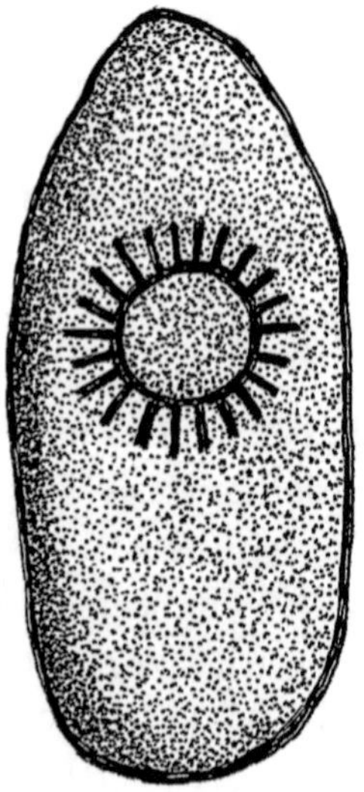

Sun image, from a statue-menhir

joy we felt seemed to indicate that we had been accepted by the elemental guardians of the site; we were being recognized for our cooperation in restoring the function of a significant feature of the ancient sacred landscape and linking it into the energetic network once again.

Rather to our surprise, the four of us then found that there were portals between some of the stones, which we were sure would now be able to function more effectively as etheric gateways for beings from other dimensions. Alain's dowsing rods swung as if a door were opening, and his pendulum dowsing confirmed that these ancient portals had been closed for a long time; we had just reactivated them. We walked between them without feeling any resistance, where previously we had sensed an unwillingness to let us pass. As we have discovered elsewhere, these are places where otherworldly beings can enter our world, bringing us greater awareness and, thereby, raise the level of our own understanding.

Interestingly, at the time all this took place, Carolyn was tuning in at her home far away in California, recalling her own earlier experiences at Kercado. Perhaps, as she did so, she drew in some renewed vitality from across the ocean for the reopening of other as-yet-unrecognized energy centers and focal points to play their part in receiving and transforming solar and cosmic energies.

Crucuno

THE FIRST TIME WE WENT TO CARNAC, we were overwhelmed by the number and magnificence of the megaliths scattered all over the region—some easily accessible, others concealed in the woods, in ruins and seldom visited. After walking the best-known alignments and spending time at the lovely menhir of Le Manio, we went looking for the Crucuno enclosure. This is a rectangular *cromlech,* standing in a field surrounded by trees and farmland near the hamlet of that name. A large dolmen rears up among the houses that have grown up around it over the years. It is now a focus for visitors, standing starkly on a patch of grass right up against an old and battered house, the stone for which most likely came from the dolmen's former entrance passage.

The Crucuno *cromlech*'s four-sided arrangement of large granite stones is known as the Quadrilateral. Open to the elements, it has never had a covering mound and differs in function and structure from dolmens, which normally have entrance corridors and one or more inner chambers. It reminded us more of the close-set stone circles standing at the ends of the great alignments. Focal places for ceremonial assemblies of the ancient people of this land, these sacred sites are invariably located upon a dowsable energy ley, or solar, line.

The Crucuno dolmen

Both the rectangle and dolmen are astronomically sited in relation to the sun, but not to the same celestial events. The Crucuno Quadrilateral is set to the cardinal points of the compass, so that its long east-west sides mark the direction of both the sunrise and sunset of the equinoxes. This remarkable siting also enables the diagonal to line up with the solstices at midwinter sunset and midsummer sunrise. It is a temple to the sun, similar to Stonehenge, where the short sides of the inner rectangle formed by the four Station Stones point to the solstices, while the long sides focus on the extreme northerly rising and most southerly setting of the moon. Such a complex geometry is only possible in rectangular form within a narrow band of latitude. Clearly both Crucuno and Stonehenge were carefully located and designed around a set of astronomical sightings, recording the celestial cycles of the year for regular celebration and attunement. *

As at Stonehenge, the Crucuno rectangle may be divided into a pair of right-angled triangles; they are known as Pythagorean triangles, although the Greek philosopher after whom they are named lived long after the setting out of these megaliths. The formula of such triangles, as we learned in school, is "the square of the hypotenuse equals the sum of the squares on the other two sides." Like the musical harmonies, they have whole-number dimensions, linking mathematics and geometry. For Pythagoras, numbers, precision, and harmony were sacred principles, and he believed that the Universe, in all its infinite complexity, had been planned. He may well be right.

Such triangulation was used in the design of the Pyramids to give a standard gradient, or the *seked;* the angle of slope (the hypotenuse) was calculated by using the height and half the base measurement (the two other sides of the triangle). Largely through his initiation by Egyptian priests into Babylonian mathematics, Pythagoras was able to establish the practical importance of this geometry and its whole-number ratios and precise angles. Until quite recently, the 3:4:5 triangle, such as the one found at Crucuno, was widely used in construction, allowing builders to make knots on a so-called Druid's chord in order to set out a right-angle on the ground. The 5:12:13 triangle, such as the one used at Stonehenge, has the interesting feature of equating lunar and solar months. The exact number of lunar months in the solar year—12.369—can be found by measuring the length of the diagonal drawn from the 3:2 division point on the five-unit side.*

The Crucuno Quadrilateral was not easy to find. On our first attempt we failed to spot it, hidden, as it was then, behind brambly hedges, barbed wire, and a thick growth of gorse. As often happens when we search for megalithic sites, we followed a muddy farm track in the rain, which led us into a seemingly empty wet field. But returning a few days later, we succeeded in finding our way to the Quadrilateral, hidden as it was by dense gorse and imbued with a feeling of abandonment.

This was a site that needed to be reactivated, a task we had been forewarned to expect, but not told where, in a channeled conversation with 'White Bull'. It was dormant; no energy pulse could be felt by pendulum dowsing around the individual stones. After tuning in and asking for Angelic guidance on how to proceed, we began to walk around in opposite directions, avoiding the overgrown brambles clutching at us, one of us winding clockwise and the other unwinding anticlockwise, both of us touching each stone in turn. Then we felt the returning of a pulse, as a polarity once more registered from stone to stone, negative at one, positive at the next, and so on round the whole group, the same alternating pattern that can be dowsed at megalithic sites around the world.

It was ticking again! The site now had a tangible vitality that had not been there when we first arrived. We were now able to make our way back to the track quite easily, using a footpath that, oddly enough, had not seemed to be there before.

Two years later, returning to check things out, we were delighted to find that we could now clearly see the upright stones from the farm track that leads out of the village. We were even more delighted to find that the enclosure had been cleared of gorse and brambles, making the approach more accessible.

---

* See *Sun, Moon, and Stonehenge: High Culture in Ancient Britain* by Robin Heath (Stoneridge, New York: Blue Stone Press, 1998).

We found the Quadrilateral still in good etheric working order. It was able to receive solar and lunar energies, and was transmitting them into the Earth's energy grid through a major ley line that crosses the southern side of the enclosure. The village, too, was showing a new vitality: old houses around the green were undergoing restoration, and their gardens were colorful with flowers and potted plants. Sadly, there was no improvement at the old dolmen, which still leans heavily against the house that has replaced its entrance corridor.

We did not know at that time why the site had been energetically closed down when we first saw it, but later we learned the story. After the French Revolution, the Breton people remained loyal to the monarchy and would not accept Napoleon. The whole area was in a state of turmoil for years, during which time the Chouans, the royalist Bretons, used the Quadrilateral for secret meetings, unaware that it was a sacred power point. It was just a remote place, ideal for plotting a counter-revolution. Eventually, the royalist uprising was put down by Napoleon's troops, but the Quadrilateral had been affected.

The intensity of an activity performed at an energy point is immediately amplified and relayed to other energy sites nearby. Besides the functions of the Crucuno site for astronomical observation and celebration throughout the year, its original purpose had been to enhance the harmonious flow of solar energy around the planet. It was certainly not intended for political unrest or for setting people one against the other. Since the potential for that was considerable, from Napoleonic times on, the Quadrilateral's powers were apparently "switched off" by the Angelic or Devic guardians of the place.

The Crucuno Quadrilateral had been sleeping since that time, and now, following the intention of our work there, has been reawakened by the local Devas or elementals. Once again it is connected to the worldwide energy grid, functioning as a sacred site and etherically protected against further misuse. It remains a place of great significance, not only because of its colorful historic past.

A few years later, we made yet another visit, this time with our friends Nicole and Alain. We found a well-cared-for, signposted, open clearing with easy access, a far cry from the overgrown group of megaliths we once had to uncover. Then it had been wet and cold; now, in complete contrast, it was a hot summer afternoon. We four were the only people there. We registered the strong impression that our work was not complete, that there still was something intangible needing to be done. Now that others had carried out the visible work of clearing the undergrowth, we sensed we were supposed to look again at what was not so easily seen. Having just been to Kercado, where we helped accomplish a perceptible restoration of the energy, it seemed to be time to try and do the same at Crucuno.

Intuitively positioning ourselves where missing stones may have stood, as we had done at Kercado, we immediately felt the energy pulling us, creating a circuit through us and around the stone rectangle. It seemed we had ratcheted up the energy already present by another notch or so, adding to our feelings of joy and exhilaration.

With his dowsing rods, Alain found portals between certain pairs of stones that surely had not been there before, indicating that a new potential had been added for Devic entities to enter the atmosphere of Earth. We remembered being told by the channeled guide "White Bull" back in England that the whole area around Carnac is a "cosmic airport," used by celestial beings wanting to help our planet and its inhabitants. They do not need mechanical spacecraft for such travel but, instead, an active portal set within an established energy center. Such nonphysical entities are usually invisible to the human eye, their frequency and wavelength being beyond our limited range of perception. Sometimes, though, the appearance of a flash of light seen from the corner of an eye will indicate their presence.

A sacred site such as Crucuno may well be continuing to serve as a communication center for such Angelic and other celestial beings. Certainly, we can say that the presence of the Nature spirits is perceptible there, even to skeptics.

Gavrinis

WE DID NOT FEEL DRAWN to the island of Gavrinis until after we had finished writing *Let The Standing Stones Speak*. Although we had received hints of its secrets during our first visit to the area, it did not seem to contain information of the kind encoded in the megaliths of the Carnac alignments. The access to Gavrinis is by sea so, like Carolyn before us, we boarded a small motorboat with a guide and a group of tourists and, wrapped up in scarves and coats against an October wind, we headed out across a choppy sea.

The only building on this tiny island is a privately owned farmhouse, near the site of a former monastic refuge for the Knights Templar. The main man-made feature of Gavrinis is its great tumulus of well-laid stones. Restored and covered in turf, as it would have been originally, the tumulus hides a fine dolmen with a long entrance passage leading to an inner chamber, large enough to hold about a dozen people. It is sited on an Athene line, one of the feminine energy bands that, along with the masculine Apollo line, link this place with other significant sites around the world, including Mont-St-Michel in France, Delphi and the Parthenon in Greece, and Avebury and Glastonbury in Britain. That serpentine energy field, which dowsing indicates emanates from the planet Jupiter, follows a sinuous interweaving course quite unlike the straight energy ley lines. It carries the consciousness-raising energies of certain Archangels and, together with the ley lines, forms part of the planetary grid system (see Chapter 9).

When the tumulus was constructed, the island of Gavrinis was still part of the mainland. Some 4,000 years ago, though, the sea level began to rise, separating it from what had once been an extensive and interconnected arrangement of megaliths. Several other small islands still have standing stones on them as well, some now underwater and exposed only at low tide.

The most intriguing thing about the tumulus, as Carolyn found years earlier, is the amount of carving on the stone slabs inside the chamber and along the passage leading to it. The multiple designs make it the most elaborately decorated known prehistoric structure in Europe. The many repetitive, swirling patterns have some similarity to the great mounds of Newgrange and nearby Knowth in Ireland, where archaeologists have recently uncovered a number of other remarkable carvings.

These beautifully worked, sophisticated designs clearly have a symbolic meaning not yet understood, and a function beyond the simply decorative. We found by dowsing that adjoining sections on some slabs carry alternate positive and nega-

Engraving on stone

tive polarities, either side of a line cut into the stone that—deliberately, it seemed to us—divided them. This phenomenon parallels the alternating polarities found from one stone to the next in stone circles, along the alignments and in other prehistoric enclosures. In fact, we even find alternating polarities when we dowse at the energy center of our own home, an old French farmhouse, where the polarity of two granite stones set into a wall reverses at the time of the full moon, leaving the other stones in the wall unaffected.

In common with the oldest dolmens in the area, the tumulus at Gavrinis is part ancestral tomb and part temple. According to archaeologists, it fell out of use five thousand years ago, when a timber structure at the entrance burned down. Its remains had been carefully covered over. It was at this extraordinary place that I encountered an Angelic presence in the form of a luminous blue light, familiar to me as the presence guiding us during the writing of our first book.

Inside the central chamber at the heart of the tumulus, our guide explained the meaning of one of the engravings. During the discussion, an elderly woman in the group kept staring at me and loudly questioning the guide's interpretation. I found her disturbing, and perhaps her challenging attitude triggered what happened next, as my mind opened up to the possibility that she might be right. Suddenly it seemed obvious to me that the designs were not about idols or mother goddesses, but were more like symbols of energy circuits, a generator of some kind with the power to transmit electric impulses. The understanding that these stones might be interactive with people has been overlooked by conventional, more objective archaeology, but all at once it became clear that this must surely be their purpose. The intense vibrations within the chamber were palpable to me, then overpowering, although none of the others seemed aware of any change in the air. After a few moments of feeling that my head was going to explode, I had to leave before it became unbearable.

Hurriedly leaving the chamber, I made my way down the long, shadowy corridor of engraved stones, one hand on them to keep my balance. I felt from each one an emanation of pulsating energy, as, struggling for breath, I made my way toward the fresh air outside. As I looked toward the entrance, a radiant light shone azure blue against the darkness of stone, as if to reassure and guide me. With its help, I was able to continue the rest of the way easily, passing through the bright light into the gray of a windy autumnal day. Relieved, I breathed deeply, my heartbeat returned to normal, and my Angelic guide vanished.

Had I not seen that Angelic vision of light, I might have assumed I was just feeling claustrophobic. But once outside, I recalled having a similar feeling in a Cornish *fogu*, another type of underground ceremonial chamber, which was once used by the Celtic people as a place of initiation. On that occasion, rather than seeing an azure light, I had clearly heard the words:

There is something you need to remember here.

Now, I began to recall past visions, and answers formed even before I could ask questions.

This was a temple for the Shining Ones, who recharged their energies here to enable them to function on Earth.

In that same manner, people now go to places of worship to recharge their connection with the Source in the hope of an empowerment or a blessing.

So priests empowered their own energy circuits and their connection with Source at these sacred stones.

Many cultures talk of these unusual priests, called in Sumerian legend the Shining Ones, emissaries from the God of Light. In Ireland they are known as the Tuatha De Danann, wise ones who traveled the Earth in ancient times, retiring to their mounds when the atmosphere of Earth became too dense to support them. As their teachings included the subject of astronomy—essential knowledge for people on Earth about how to live in harmony with their environment—these messengers of Light have also been referred to as astronomer-priests, or the Old Ones.*

Then the words came to me:

The patterns on the stones were not laboriously carved by hand but created by the power of intention, via a process of thought focused like a laser beam to incise the stones with precision. It was the Shining Ones, the ones not of this planet, who had the ability to do this.

That visit to Gavrinis stirred new thoughts and insights. Of all the dolmens we were to see after that, it was only the oldest, such as the tumulus at Gavrinis, that appear to retain that mysterious connection with the Shining Ones.

---

* See *The Shining Ones* by Christian and Barbara Joy O'Brien (Cirencester, UK: Dianthus Publishing, 1997).

Part Two

9

Natasha

"The Many-Splendoured Thing"

MORE BOOKS ABOUT ANGELS are available each year, responding to a real demand for information about these celestial beings. Certainly, a growing number of people are aware of the existence of Angels, many of them through their own experiences; however, when Francis Thompson wrote his poem and referred to the Angelic realm as *The Many-Splendoured Thing*, scepticism was the order of the day.

There are still many people who are unable to believe in Angels and, even if they accept the idea, wonder about the physical details; what could an Angel possibly be doing all day? Where do they live? Is it in a parallel world from which they look down upon us from on high, clad in billowing robes, soaring on feathered wings, as in medieval paintings? Or perhaps they exist as an extension of our own world but in a dimension normally invisible to us?

It is, however, a place that the mystics of old seem to have visited on several occasions. According to Biblical patriarch Enoch, presumed author of the famous book of Angelic revelations, for example, the faces of the Angels "...shone like the sun, and their eyes burned like lamps," describing the beings he encountered when he was apparently transported to a higher dimension.

Many of us equate Angels with the fairy-tales of childhood. As adults, we leave all that behind, unable to see their relevance to the happenings and difficulties of daily life. Today's culture, with its emphasis on technology and the material world, provides an interpretation of life that for a long time has excluded the Angelic realm, unseen as it usually is. Nevertheless, it once helped our world come into being—and it continues to exist in parallel with it, whether we now believe in it or not.

Long before the birth of Jesus Christ, a science called Angelology was formulated by the Essenes of Palestine, groups of ascetics for whom communion with Angels was a natural part of their daily life. The Essenes had developed this understanding from the teachings of Enoch. To them (and to Enoch), the Angelic

Sun and Angels, Quintanilla de las Viñas, Spain

kingdom was the creative force of the Universe, which expressed itself in the physical world in the four elements of Earth, Fire, Air and Water, in the alchemy of Nature. In the medieval era, the differing characteristics of that creative energy were attributed to the Archangels, who were given names that we continue to use today.

The splendid Angelic realm continues to affect us directly and continuously, illuminating and invigorating our lives, if only we would notice. Specifically, we receive its influence in the form of planetary radiations, an energetic network that is wrapped protectively around the Earth. Long known to the American Indians as Grandmother Spider's web, and recognized in many other traditions worldwide, it is an interlacing network of energy that has come to be called the planetary grid system. It provides a framework to carry the many facets of the life force and actively supports all living things on our planet.

In fact, it is a global network of influences that come from the sun and the planets of the solar system. As in the Kabbalistic Tree of Life of the esoteric Hebrew tradition, each of these is associated with the particular qualities of an Archangel; that is to say, with certain attributes of the Divine. It is from those dynamics that we derive aspects of our own being.

Those associations also formed part of the teaching of the Essene mystery schools, which were once active in Egypt and Palestine and some of whose writings survive in the scrolls found in the Qumran caves near the Dead Sea, popularly known as The Gnostic Gospels. The Essene Tree of Life has seven heavenly branches above and seven earthly roots below, the roots and branches resembling rays of the sun, with the human being halfway between.

Essene Tree of Life

The concept of the Tree of Life originates in the world of Spirit, and is usually applied to our physical world as a symbol of the energy fields that affect us. Both the Hebrew and Essene descriptions of the Tree of Life may be extended, up or down, to illustrate other levels of energetic life of which we may be unaware.

In the Hebrew model of the Universe, the Archangels are each associated with a planet and occupy ten *sefiroth,* or containers of light, on the Tree of Life, the meaning of which can only be summarized here in the briefest form. They are linked by a flow of energy that derives from the Highest Source of Light at the Crown, the topmost point on the central pillar, or trunk of the Tree, which represents Equilibrium. Within the Crown are placed Archangel Metatron and the Shekinah, the male and female aspects of Divinity. Below it is an empty space to indicate the Holy Spirit, or that which is not manifest, the Divine Source from which all knowledge is derived. At the center of that pillar is the sun—the power of Archangel Michael—as the focal point, and below that Gabriel, the Messenger. At the base of the Tree of Life is Earth, with its guardian Archangel Sandalphon, who also has a female counterpart known as Auriel or Uriel. Metatron may be said to represent pure energy, while Sandalphon represents the energy that is manifest on Earth. Human souls have the task of moving from their incarnation at the lowest level, up the central pillar toward the Divine Source at the Crown.

Of the two outer pillars, one represents Expansion or activity, the other Contraction or passivity, and each bears three more of these Archangelic archetypes. The whole symbolic pattern, which can also be related to the main organs or energy centers in the human body, was impressed onto a Wiltshire field in the summer of 1997, making use of the farmer's tractor tramlines, as a remarkably precise crop circle.

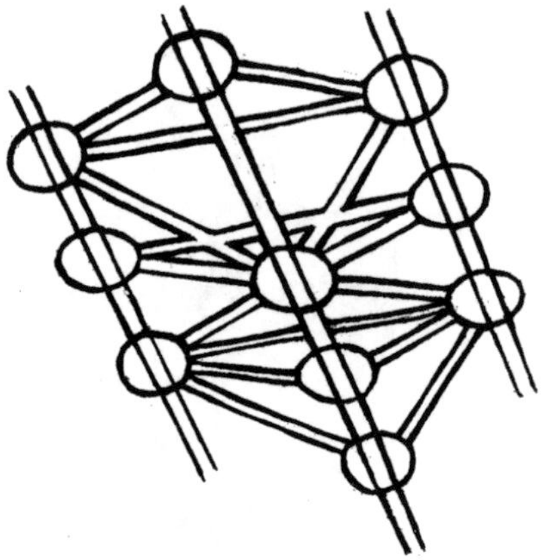

Tree of Life crop circle

The characteristic qualities of each Archangel are carried to Earth as radiations of power from the planet with which each one is linked. The imprint upon Earth of those radiations is a worldwide network of linear patterns and energies that can be detected and measured. Not usually visible, they seem to be comparable to natural vibratory fields such as magnetic and electrical, and to man-made fields such as radio and television.

Considerable research throughout the twentieth century, especially in Germany and Russia, has confirmed the existence of much of this planetary grid, each field or network being found to have a distinct pattern, flow, and dimension. Bearing the names of those who first identified them, these fields include the close-set Hartmann and Curry grids, and the larger Peyré, Wittmann, and Schneider grids, or lattices. Others clearly exist, but as yet are unnamed. Each one has a rectangular or diamond pattern and a different dimension; they can be found by dowsing virtually everywhere, on the ground, over the ocean, even from an aeroplane. The influence of this universal network upon the Earth, and all its life-forms, cannot be underestimated. Moreover, it is flexible, which is to say the lattices seem to breathe, expanding and contracting in response to human attention, the vibrations of sound, music, and even thought. I have created a simplified table that indicates the links that seem to exist among these grids of energy, the Archangels, and the celestial bodies of our solar system.

These dowsable patterns seem, however, to be excluded from ancient places of burial, such as the dolmen mounds. This was presumably by human agency, by

Planet/Star	Name	Archangel	Description/meters
Sun	Energy Ley	Michael	straight *
Moon	Hartmann	Uriel	rectangular 2 x 2
Neptune	Curry	Zaphkiel	diamond 3.5 x 3.5
Pluto	Peyré	Metatron	rectangular 5 x 5
Venus	Wittmann	Raphael	diamond 16 x 16
Mercury	Broad Curry	Gabriel	diamond 100 x 100
Uranus	—	Raziel	diamond, large
Mars	Schneider	Hanael	diamond, larger
Saturn	—	Samael	diamond, very large
Jupiter	Apollo/Athena	Zadkiel	curving pair, random

Dimensions vary with latitude but are approximate for Northern Europe.
* May conform to the UVG Grid pattern.

an early priesthood who understood that souls can become trapped on the Earth plane by certain energy fields, and even travel along ley lines; instead, the shape of each burial mound is delineated by a serpentine line, which then meanders over the landscape to link with the next mound. This may have been intended to free the souls of the dead for release to another dimension and guided their journey to a sacred site, where ritual celebration by ancient peoples would have taken place at the appropriate time, between the autumn equinox and the winter solstice.

Most generally known are the straight energy ley lines, bands that we understand as bearing the all-important solar, rather than planetary, energy. They also extend over the Earth, linking sacred places and ancient sites, some of which are unmarked, many others identifiable by the megaliths, churches, mosques, and temples that have been sited on them over the centuries. Flowing in straight alignments of varying widths, many of the wider ley lines have been mapped and named in recent years. It is possible, but not yet fully researched, that they conform to a complex spherical pattern, known as the UVG Grid (which can be viewed on the Google Earth Web site). Based upon the three-dimensional geometry of the Platonic solids, the UVG Grid is a refinement of an earlier Russian theory of an overall geometric pattern to the energy ley lines.

There is also another planetary emanation with a different imprint upon our globe. As far as we know, it comes from Jupiter, the largest planet in the solar system, and bears the characteristics of the Archangels Zadkiel and Zaphkiel. Unlike the other networks, which are straight and have a latticelike pattern, it has no discernible geometry. It consists of twin curving bands of energy, one having positive polarity, the other negative, that sweep across the landscape, sometimes crossing at significant places, in a fashion that is apparently random. They are known as the Apollo and Athena currents from their presence at classical Greek temples with those dedications or as Michael and Mary currents in other parts of Europe, because they are found at churches so dedicated.* In China they are identified as Dragon Lines and are part of the Feng Shui tradition.

All megalithic monuments, and most old places of worship of whatever kind or belief, are sited upon one or another of these many dowsable patterns of solar and Jupiter energy that criss-cross every country on Earth. Such precise placement of man-made structures in the ancestral landscape was of great importance to those who set them up. It shows also that dowsing ability, as we call it now, was once widespread, and not necessarily the preserve of shamans, priests, or the medieval master-masons. That ability to perceive and pinpoint the flow and nodal points of cosmic energy is almost lost today, yet it remains inherent in each one of us. Curiously, all the crop circles that appear each year—mainly in Britain, but also in many other countries—are located on these lines of energy, a possible indication of their mysterious source.

Our relationship with the Angelic and all unseen levels of being is clearly complex. The ancient Greeks turned the Archangels into gods (such as Zadkiel, who became Zeus) who displayed human attributes—many of them negative—that they used as guidelines for their own behavior, creating myths and legends of heroic adventures based on the motions of celestial spheres.

Astrology has long told us that all human lives are subject to planetary influences—animals and plants, too. Recent scientific studies have noted periodic changes in the growth buds of trees and plant life at the time each planet in its orbit lines up with Earth and the moon, because each species has its own allegiance, as it were, to a particular planet. The oak, for instance, relates to Mars, the willow to the moon, the yew to Saturn, and so on.

The entire planetary web can be seen as the extension of a Universal, creative intelligence, which informs the Earth and all of life and is overseen by the Archangels, who have an unbroken contract with the Creator to watch over our planet.

Angels have been known throughout history to make themselves evident in

---

* See *The Sun and the Serpent,* by Hamish Miller and Paul Broadhurst (Pendragon Press, 1990) and *The Dance of the Dragon,* Pendragon Press, by the same authors.

troubled times, in dreams or visions, giving guidance when it is most needed. Since we have ignored so much of importance for so long, and may soon have to face the consequences, we are being invited now to consciously open ourselves to their presence. The life force that informs every being, every form, every stone, comes from the Creative Source of the Universe (or whatever other label you prefer), and is mediated by the Archangels. That energy flow is neutral; how we make use of it is our choice.

Our connection with the celestial spheres is one that we cannot live without, whether we are aware of it or not. We can use it wisely to fulfil our potential and inspire other people, or we can direct it to egocentric ends, which will ultimately cause suffering to ourselves and to the generations to come. If we fail to make positive and conscious use of this connection, with some understanding of the knowledge taught in all the early mystery schools (many of which actually existed prior to Enoch's revelations), we cannot expect to live in health or harmony with each other, or with our environment.

Since Angelic guidance is available to all of us at all times, one might think that, with the increase in the world's population, there would not be enough Angels to go round. But as "many-splendoured" beings from another realm, their existence is not limited to a single dimension. They are capable of manifesting in many places at the same time without diminution of their powers. Indeed, it would appear that the opposite occurs—as more people call upon the Angelic hosts, the greater their power becomes.

When humans forget to call upon Angels, whether through disbelief, ignorance, or fear, there is no input of that Higher Power to help us find solutions to man-made problems. Even as our problems increase, it is becoming less likely that they will be resolved unless we ask for help from the higher level of awareness that has such an immeasurably wider perspective than our own.

Indian sage Krishnamurti said:

> Thought has created disorder... Thought is matter. It is of the material world... We are trying to find an answer to the major problems of our human life through the operation of thought... Thought has not found an answer, and it never will.

Christian doctrine once recognized the contribution of Angels to our earthly existence; however, from the fourth century onward, the Church excluded beings of the Angelic realm, out of concern that they would become objects of idolatrous worship. The belief did not die, of course; it was quietly transferred to mythology.

In the Jewish belief system, though, the Kabbalah has long been understood as a revelation from the Archangel Uriel and is largely concerned with their attributes and planetary connections. Similarly, in Islam, the Holy Book, or Koran, is accepted as dictation from the Archangel Jibril, or Gabriel.

I often meet people who, when talking with me about their work—frequently as much to do with social interaction, education, and healing therapies, as with creativity—tell me how much better it goes when they ask for help from the Angelic realm. Even the Master Jesus said, "On my own I am nothing." The medieval mystic, Hildegarde of Bingen, experienced visions of Angels that inspired her writings and paintings; she received information about cures for medical problems that is still accepted and has been scientifically proven to be of value. There are other well-known examples from more recent times. Poet William Blake was well acquainted with Angelic presences, which animated his life and many visionary works; the Swedish mystic Swedenborg had visions of Angels; and the influential philosopher Rudolf Steiner well understood the significance of Angels and the elemental spirits of Nature and once saw Angels around standing stones in Wales.

It would appear that the Archangels' objective is to raise the level of human awareness, by helping to widen our perception of the invisible realm, the parallel world of Spirit that lies behind and yet permeates our lives. Our human actions have consequences in the world of Spirit, as well as in our physical world. Our lack of conscious cooperation with that process seems to have had a detrimental effect on those higher levels, as well as on our own planet and ourselves, since we are all interconnected.

Yet always, and at any moment, we have the possibility to allow enlightenment into our lives through an understanding of the wisdom that has always been available, and an intelligent awareness of the outcome of our own thoughts and actions. It is through those thoughts and activities that Angels are attracted to our human energy field. This is especially the case with our intentions, for Angels can as easily read our aura as a butterfly or a bee reads the ultraviolet pattern in a flower petal.

Different Angelic resonances will accord with our intentions, so that in working with a difficult mathematical problem we might feel inspired by Uriel, who is concerned with forms of creative construction, while Raphael may be drawn to assist healers. Ultimately, there is no division, only different layers of Creation, since, as we know from quantum physics, everything in the Universe is interconnected at the most basic subatomic or particle level—energetic motion, which for us coalesces into matter. Despite "appearances" there is no separation, and our conscious or unconscious intentions affect everything around us.

There are books about "cosmic ordering," or asking the Universe for what you want. This is nothing new: the human race has been doing this for a very long time, often unconsciously, as a result of fear or negative thought forms, which tend to continue the pattern of problems in people's lives. The difference now is that we are coming to realize that if our thoughts are directed toward more positive outcomes, with a certain lightness of heart, and combined with actions that also work toward the desired end, they will together assist us in obtaining Angelic help for our projects, even for our health. What we wish for, or intend, may well transpire, because we are actively and positively attracting it. This can turn ordinary or problematic events into "inspired happenings," or something we call "out of the ordinary."

We had an experience while traveling through France, when intuition, which did not make sense at the time, led us to a town with a golden Angel as its symbol. Usually we make a hotel reservation for one night, allowing us to divide our journey into a couple of enjoyable days. This gives us enough time to explore anything interesting en route, without having to spend time looking for accommodation. This time, though, we failed to reserve a room at the quiet hotel by the river, which had often been our previous refuge; we'll find somewhere else for a change, just as pleasant, we thought.

After some hours of traveling, dusk began to fall, and it was time to find a place to stay. As we were not far from our usual stopping place, I had an inclination to go there. Following the quiet country road by the river, we were overtaken by a sports car, which raced noisily past. The hotel is near a racing circuit, so we took that as an obvious signal that the place might be full. "We'll go there anyway," I said, following my feelings. We parked at the hotel and were just leaving the car when the owner came over to say she was sorry, they were indeed full—as was everywhere else, she added. My hopes were dashed, we were tired, and I wondered why I had felt guided to come here at all. "Can you suggest anywhere else," I asked, hopefully. She looked uncertain, then said: "Ah yes, but it is a half-hour drive from here. It's called Le Dorat, and there you will find a room".

Setting off into the gathering darkness, I realized we had called there simply to be told about Le Dorat. We both felt that it would be so good to arrive at a place where we might seem to be expected, like friends coming to visit, somewhere welcoming with a comfortable room, pleasant view, and a good meal, and that was the request I put to our invisible Angelic friends.

Reaching Le Dorat, we parked in a small side street and walked around. A hotel that looked promising was closed, another looked a bit gloomy, then we saw a little card in the window of a big old house. It read simply, "For bed and breakfast, ring the bell." Through the glass, we saw a woman in long flowing skirts. She opened the door. I asked if there was a room available. With a soft Scottish accent, she said, "Yes, and you are very welcome." Then she showed us up an old wooden staircase to a delightful room with an enchanting view over the old town.

Later, over a glass of wine, she and her husband told us that Le Dorat means the Gilded One, named after the life-sized golden Angel that stands atop the local abbey, long a place of pilgrimage. All the restaurants were closed, so we were invited to have a meal with our hosts and spent a most enjoyable evening with them. The next day, we explored the town, admired the old quarter and fine medieval houses, and gazed up at the lofty, gleaming Angel. Silently thanking our invisible helpers, we left. We had made new friends.

A small experience, perhaps, but for us a meaningful and delightful one.

10

Carolyn

Miracles do not happen in contradiction to Nature,
but only in contradiction to what is known in Nature.
—ST AUGUSTINE

Communication

SEVERAL YEARS AGO my husband was diagnosed with prostate cancer and we were told he would need three months of daily radiation treatments. It had been more than fifteen years since my trip to Carnac, and I was still exploring how sound could be used for healing, so I tried singing to him. For five months, from diagnosis to the end of the radiation period, I sang my improvisations to him every evening in my studio.

I sang the tones and melodies I heard in my mind's ear and asked for help from whatever guides might be there to help us, paying attention to the images, insights, and ideas that came through, as I had once done at the stones in Brittany.

The experience was like dreaming while awake, and the voices I heard were, if anything, more insistent than they had been those many years earlier. I was encouraged to keep careful notes and to understand that "healing" and "teachings" were one and the same. The more I understood the basics of where healing came from and why it worked, the more effective I would be when I let go and just sang.

During those five months of singing every evening, I learned about energy and matter and form; about DNA and family patterns; about fear and ignorance and how all of this relates to cancer cells. My impromptu songs became the sounds of the teachings themselves and the currents upon which my prayers could ride. Singing for this man I loved so well, I could sing love right into his cells, encouraging wholeness in his afflicted system.

I cannot claim to understand this process—neither then, with my husband, nor two decades earlier at the stones; however, in both cases, I mysteriously received unbidden information from I knew not where, spoken to me directly by some intelligence that knew me well and wished to help. Although I had no idea from whom or from where these messages were coming, I trusted them. They "rang all my bells," and convinced me that they were true by their clarity, their deep logic, and the exciting new information they conveyed. The most important thing is that it worked! In three months of radiation treatments, my husband lost neither his appetite nor a day of work and had no side effects nor aftereffects. The doctors did not know how to account for this.

Of course, the hearing of so-called "spirit voices" is not unique to Natasha and me. Not only have indigenous peoples courted these spirits since time immemorial but anyone who has read the Bible will recognize variants of the same story in the "still, small voice" of the Lord coming through the tempest, in Noah being instructed to build an Ark, in St. Paul hearing the voice on the road to Damascus, in the Archangel Gabriel reciting the text of the Koran to the Prophet Mohammad. In fact, most of the world's great religions are based upon such revelations coming from the unseen world.

Indigenous cultures have thrived since the beginning of human presence on the planet, and all are dependent upon the ability of certain individuals to enter altered states of consciousness in which otherworldly beings are contacted for their wisdom. This wisdom is then brought back for the healing and edification of their communities. Those who do this work—the so-called shamans—have ways of accessing a deep state of knowledge from "other realms" for the betterment of everybody. They are revered as the medicine people of their communities.

The words "altered state" only mean that no part of the natural abilities of the mind are repressed; that the normally censored aspects of our consciousness are free to be present. In societies such as our own, this uncensored state is mistrusted and considered dangerous; it can even be punishable as a criminal offense!

The techniques for achieving this state include plant sacraments, rhythmic dancing and chanting, and forms of sensory deprivation, commonly called "techniques of ecstasy." The ecstatic experience is available to everyone. During such experiences, we know the joy of being in immediate communion with the consciousness of the whole world. The grand scheme of the Universe is as available to us as is the perfect beauty of a tiny flower. We just have to recognize that ecstasy is our birthright.

This implies, of course, that consciousness is not something we produce in our minds but, rather, it is already intrinsic to ourselves and the world we live in. It is like an ocean in which we swim. In other words, we participate in a conscious world; we do not create consciousness. To some 2 percent of the population, the so-called "altered state" seems to come naturally without the help of external stimulants. Perhaps Natasha and I are amongst those intuitive listeners whose receptors are naturally attuned to receiving the messages in the air around us—here, there, and everywhere.

Here, there, and everywhere... a larger field of consciousness? What might these phrases really mean? According to ancient wisdom traditions from all over the world, ultimately everything in our Universe comes from an all-encompassing Oneness that contains everything in existence, through all Space and Time and beyond, visible and invisible. We humans are aware of the physical world we live in—the Earth and its wonders, the plants and animals and people—but many of us do not know that we also have access to an unseen world, often referred to as the Spirit World (for want of a better term). This is where we imagine the elves and faeries and Angels to abide, where the ancestors can be found. We imagine it as a place, but perhaps it is nowhere else but right here, right now. The frequency is different, that's all.

In indigenous cultures this Spirit World—this otherworld—was contacted on a regular basis for assistance in healing the members of the tribe, for bringing rain, for connecting with the ancestors. The membrane between the worlds was thin, just a shift of consciousness away in the same world in which they lived, but was always reachable.

Such indigenous societies sustained themselves successfully for at least 35,000 years. In less than two hundred years, our modern materialistic societies have managed to degrade the Earth, imperil plant and animal species, and threaten our continued existence. Children go hungry, our air and water is fouled, human beings war against each other and live in an ongoing state of fear. Might there be a correlation here?

It would be hard to argue that there is not.

During the time I was singing for my husband and receiving information about his condition, I was also given to understand that the DNA that resides in every living cell on Earth is the means by which life receives the intelligence of the Universe itself. The images I received were of intelligent energy streaming in from every direction and every dimension of the whole Cosmos, being stepped down into material form for transmission into individual living beings via their DNA, the transformer of the energy.

DNA enabled the consciousness of the Source to be differentiated into the physical world, plant and animal, and into different species and individual lifeforms, from bacteria to redwood trees to human beings. What the biologists call "Junk DNA" is, of course, no such thing; its function is simply not yet understood. If anything, we might call it "blessed, mysterious DNA."

Our DNA is very likely the doorway through which communication between the worlds takes place, including the messages that Natasha and I—and many others—have been fortunate enough to receive. Only ten atoms wide, DNA is so tiny it sits at that ephemeral divide between visible and invisible existence. Our ability to communicate through that divide most likely depends upon our ability to, first, recognize that we live in more than just a physical, mechanistic Universe; and second, that Nature is a conscious, living whole, of which we are one of its forms of expression.

Once we can accept that we are not alone in the Universe, we may begin to learn how to listen for the guidance that is waiting for us to ask for its assistance. Hopefully, we will be wise enough to ask. Then we may hear what steps need to be taken in order for us to save ourselves and protect our world from the devastation we have so mindlessly courted.

Ritual

FROM TIME IMMEMORIAL, American Indian pueblos all over New Mexico have held ritual Corn Dances in the late summer shortly before the harvest, to bring rain. This tradition has continued unbroken, even through the Christianization of New Mexico. The Corn Dance is one of the largest sacred ceremonies still practiced in that region, and one of the few open to the public. The all-day event is an extraordinary spectacle, featuring row upon row of brightly dressed traditional dancers, representing the deities known as *kachinas*, the supernatural intermediaries between the Creator Spirit and the Peoples of the Earth. The kachinas make their home in the mountains in winter and return to the pueblos every July to assist Pueblo people in ensuring a good harvest.

During the summer of 2007, while visiting friends in New Mexico, I was taken to one of these annual Corn Dances at a pueblo near Albuquerque. On the way there, my friends told me a story from the Hopi oral tradition, about how all the knowledge of the world was once known to all the beings: people, animals, stones, plants. Everything in the Cosmos was conscious, everything in the Cosmos was connected, and everything was held in balance. When things became out of balance, the people would hold a dance ceremony to recalibrate themselves with the Earth and the Heavens, and all would again be in tune.

Well, at some point, so the story goes, things got so out of balance the truth of wholeness was lost, and so each clan was given one portion of the truth to hold onto until the time came for all the separate pieces to be brought back together again. But even that got lost over time, and in these days people do not remember that each clan knows only one portion of the whole truth. The Hopi, my friends told me, say that the time has come for us to choose between keeping the truth divided, and thus destroying the planet and ourselves, and reuniting all the pieces and restoring the balance of life.

As we came to the pueblo's dancing grounds—a long, narrow plaza surrounded by multistory adobe dwellings and underground ceremonial chambers known as *kivas*—the sun was climbing into a cloudless sky, already spreading its heat into the dust of the windless southwestern desert. People with umbrellas were taking their places on the verandas and rooftops of the adobes, at the bases of the kivas, and wherever else they could find a bit of shade. The people closest to the dancers, seated in the first row were, I noticed, the elderly, the disabled, and the children. Everyone made room for them, giving them choice places in the shade.

These honorees were also the first to be approached by the *koshari*, the clown kachinas, who entered the plaza and went directly to people seated in the front row, offering them greetings, jokes, and gifts of pine boughs. When, as an outsider, I was also handed a fragrant bit of pine by one of the mud-painted koshari, I was moved to be so welcomed into this indigenous ritual ("indigenous" meaning "belonging in a place, belonging to a lineage"), where we would all be entering sacred space and sacred time together.

These koshari, whose near-naked bodies were daubed with the local clay, whose breech-cloths hung with foxtails and clattering shells and whose heads were crowned with corn husks would, my friends informed me, behave like clowns throughout the ceremony. They would provide a kind of "crazy wisdom," acting outrageously, teasing and provoking laughter. It was the koshari way of teaching moderation, I was told. Their function was to keep everyone's spirits up, to provide cookies and sips of water to the dancers, to help when people's costumes came undone, and to keep a general eye out for the wellbeing of the community.

A hypnotic throbbing of drums and deep male chanting reached us from a distance, growing stronger as a line of men with big drums entered the plaza, their presence immediately consecrating the bare, dusty space. Solemnly, they took their place at one end, establishing the beat that would continue unbroken for the next eight hours, preparing the community to participate with their prayers for a successful ritual Corn Dance.

The drummers seemed to create a time out of time, a space deeper than the world. We watchers were carried by the drumbeats into a state that was relaxed and yet alert, and sitting back against the adobe wall I entered into my own quiet place. By the time all the dancers had filed into the plaza, line after line of hundreds of men, women, children, and elders in elaborate costumes and moccasined feet, I was fairly hypnotized. Colors waved in front of my eyes and figures bobbed up and down in their rhythmic shuffling dance as the lines crossed and zig-zagged, shifted and swayed. The beat was augmented by the shells and rattles worn on waists and ankles, and the plaza became a pulsing wash of sound and color, mesmerizing me and everyone around me.

Suddenly I was back in Carnac, seeing the dance among the stones on that foggy morning looking down from the Tumulus St-Michel. That had been vision, but this was reality, happening right now, here in my own country! The scene, though, was the same: a community of people dancing in lines to the hypnotic beat of drums and chants, re-tuning to each other and to the world. I recognized it from that vision years before at the stones; it was the same! People dancing to attune with the Earth and Heaven, to heal as a community and be initiated into universal laws. By reaffirming to each other their sacred connection to all of existence, they were maintaining the world.

"They never speak to outsiders about the real meaning of these dances," my friends told me, "but each dancer is selected and trained by the elders from a baby. It is a lifelong learning, and they consider us outsiders to be ignorant of the deeper significance of what they do and how they do it."

I imagined those other long-ago people by the sea in France being taught from childhood to read the subtle signals of the stones, to feel the reciprocating pulse in their own bodies and to gather at auspicious times to dance and sing, as they worked together to ensure collective balance with each other and with the Earth.

We watched the dance in the plaza for more than six hours. As the sun rose higher in the sky, the beat never stopped, even as the dancers and singers periodically filed out of the plaza to rest and another group just as large replaced them. The koshari skip-hopped through the lines, encouraging everyone's efforts, especially the little ones, and the young men wildly shook their rattles whenever the beat, from one end of the plaza to the other, grew ragged. The dancers responded by bringing their feet sharply back to the common pulse, following an ancient pattern passed down since the beginning of the world.

It was their faces that especially fascinated me, as the dancers passed close to us on the sidelines, then moved away, continuing forward, then swinging into the diagonal as they zig-zagged in the other direction. They barely noticed us or even each other. I saw no sign of strain, no self-consciousness. Their eyes seemed to look inward, lips relaxed, their brows smooth. The young men, their energy vigorous even as the sweat streamed from bare, muscled chests, never showed a sign of bravado or competition. All I saw was focus and simple commitment to the ritual—even the children—a tribe of people with a single purpose to align with the Earth and Sky, to bring balance between the human community and the gods, to bring the needed rain that would feed the crops that, for the rest of the year, would feed them.

From time to time during the daylong ceremony, as the sun rose higher into a sky that remained absolutely cloudless, I would slip out of the plaza to meander through the back lanes of the pueblo, where ordinary life was happening. Kids in tee-shirts chased each other, babies cried, women visited and cooked, and resting dancers milled about in their elaborate costumes, smoking and eating. Surrounded by the ordinariness of everyday life, I found my mind shifting back to its habitual chatter of noticing and wondering, judging and thinking, as my body let me know it was hungry, thirsty, tired.

After locating the outhouses and munching on fry bread, I would duck back into the plaza again, where my mind would slow way down, my body would feel again the steady beat of the drums, and my eyes would go soft with the moving colors of the dancers. I was back in no-time, where the world spread softly and a borderless space cushioned me. I was again part of the Mystery.

La participation mystique. I recognized it and let myself relax and focus along with the dancers and singers. As the day wore on, each time I returned to the plaza from the outskirts it took less time for my body to reenter sacred space, and each time I left, it was harder to leave the ceremony behind. I felt the way a fish must feel when stranded on dry land by a rogue wave, after the ease of the ocean.

It reminded me of a time I had accompanied a friend to the hospital and, during her treatment, had strolled out to the hospital's roof garden to wait for her. The only other person there was an elderly Chinese gentleman standing in prayer before one of the potted magnolias placed on the tar and gravel. Then he began to move. He raised his arms, circled them above his head, brought them to his chest, and bowed to the magnolia, exhaling audibly before rising again, lifting his arms, bowing and breathing. He repeated this ritual for most of an hour while I watched mesmerized, and he only stopped when a doctor came out onto the roof to find him. With one last bow to the magnolia in the planter, he calmly followed the doctor back to the recovery room where, no doubt, his loved one lay.

Here, beneath the clear blue sky of the Southwest desert, I seemed to be witnessing a similar ritual on a much grander scale. That Chinese man had been invoking the natural world—via a small tree in a pot of earth—in supplication for the welfare of one person. This large community in the New Mexican desert was invoking the same powers of the Universe to bring rain for the fields of corn that would sustain them all. In both cases, they seemed to be matching their own frequencies of vibration to those of the natural world to find the point of resonance between the human and the Divine.

As the shadows grew longer, that resonance grew ever more palpable among those of us in the plaza, the dancers and the watchers. Our own hearts, on the sidelines, entrained to the same rhythms of the drumbeats and footfalls. Deep longings in myself—longings of which I had been unaware—were being addressed and comforted as I participated in this profound bonding ritual. I had felt it all before on that fogbound morning in Carnac, seeing those ghostly dancers bobbing up and down the rows of standing stones. What I believe I had witnessed there, and now in real time in the Southwest desert, was an ancient spiritual technology to align the human with the cosmic, the Earth with the Divine. It made so much sense. How could modern culture have forgotten this?

The sun dipped toward the western horizon, and still the sky remained blue and cloudless. The dancers danced in their moving lines, and the drumbeat kept up its steady beats. Some of the younger children had dropped out of the dance and now sat among us with their relatives, but the elders I had noticed earlier were still dancing. The koshari watched out for them, peering into faces and offering sips of water, tying loose moccasin strings and shouting out teasing jokes to keep the energy high, while the singers' voices sounded loud and clear and the drumbeat never changed.

We were hot and exhausted from just sitting there all day. After eight hours, my friends gazed up at the blue sky, we checked our watches and considered leaving. We still had a long drive ahead of us to get back home. Many had already left and the crowd was thinner than it had been. The dust churned up by the dancers' feet choked the air, but not one dancer had lost focus. Who were we to tire out when they did not? So we settled back down and I closed my eyes and, leaning my sweaty back against the adobe, I went into a half-doze.

I entered a dreamtime in which time itself ceased; drumbeats became the beat of the world, this place was home, where I belonged, and the people surrounding me on every side were family. We breathed the same air, partook of the same sounds and colors, and our bodies softened and melted in a shared heat. For how long this dreamtime lasted I cannot say, but I was brought out of it— we all were— by a faraway rumble of thunder followed by another, closer.

Suddenly wide awake, we all turned eastward to face the far-off mountains, where the sky had darkened and forks of lightening bolted out in jagged streaks above backlit peaks.

Not one dancer changed pace; not one expression registered either surprise or triumph, but every foot continued its shuffling dance. The drumbeats neither wavered nor quickened, nor did the singing change its force. Headdresses bobbed up and down, as they had all day, and shells and bells clattered in perfect rhythm. Footfalls continued in the deep dust of the plaza as dark clouds heavy with rain surged toward us from afar, growing larger moment by moment. These clouds loomed huge and black and piled one upon the other. Thunder clashed and streaks of light screamed out of them as the air grew cold, the sun was eclipsed, and out of the sky came the first huge drops of pelting rain!

In seconds, we were standing in puddles, the dust of the plaza transformed into red mud. Water gushed out of the *canales* on the adobe walls, and people ran for cover. The wind blew umbrellas inside out, and plastic forks and spoons tumbled in the air. People hung onto their straw hats and laughed, exclaiming at the miracle. Yet again, the miracle! Some sought shelter, while others raised their faces to the driving rain.

The dancers and drums, however, simply came to stillness and calmly stood in lines, four and five abreast, and got rained on. They stood there quietly, getting soaked, their fur and feathers and cornhusks and clay paint dripping. The water rose above their moccasins, their headdresses drooped, but they looked neither to the left nor the right, nor did they give each other high fives or wave to their relatives in triumph. They just stood there quietly in the rain.

It was only after most of the people had left, and the older men of the tribe had entered the kiva to sit in the rain on the kiva roof, that the dancers quietly broke their ranks and, one by one, filed out of the plaza in silence.

11

Carolyn

My Stones

I HAVE HAD AN AFFINITY WITH STONES—small ones, of course, not megaliths—for as long as I can remember. As a child, certain stones seemed magical to me and, nose to the ground, I searched them out. Whenever I found one, it made me happy for days.

I kept these special stones in a secret stash, and when someone I knew was sick I would leave a stone, like a prayer, behind a nearby bush or in their mailbox. Actually, I still do. Over the years I have left hundreds of these "prayer stones" everywhere I go; they have been plunked into lakes, dropped in ditches, tucked into the roots of a tree. I would love to be there when some future geologist found one of my river stones on a lava flow in Hawaii!

But aside from this ongoing game I play, there is another category of stones in my life: the stones to which I have been led, stones that live with me and help me do my work. In the course of the past forty years, I have found—or been found by—five such stones that have come to me. This happened only when I was when I was in the midst of doing other things, never actively searching. *Pick me up,* the stone seemed to say.

The first of these special stones came to me during a winter walk on Ocean Beach in San Francisco in the 1960s, when the Vietnam War dragged on and the San Francisco Bay Area was the center of protest, hippie culture, and the Summer of Love. It was a time of hope, horror, and confusion and, as a young mother of three small children, I was greatly in need of a steady calming influence. On the beach that day, tossed up by the winter surf, were piles of stones and driftwood knotted together by long strands of seaweed—a winter beach.

The children were playing in the sand, and my husband and I were sitting gazing out at the surf, talking softly, when my fingers closed idly upon a smooth stone at my side. It was a smooth gray oblong, just the size of my palm, and when I

Small stones

looked closely I saw an uncanny column of tiny fossils embedded on its face. Each fossil was different. They lined up perfectly, one atop the other, like the energy centers of the body. I counted the fossils: seven.

I took it home with me and ever since, have held it on sleepless nights for its calming effect. When I am anxious or hurting I reach for it, and when the stone gets hot in my hand, I take that as a signal to spread its healing heat by sending prayers into the world.

I found the second extraordinary stone several years later in a dry riverbed in India, where we were living for the year. We had stopped one day to picnic beneath a *peepul* tree by a wide, dry riverbed in Madhya Pradesh. The riverbed was a jumble of dusty river rocks that would, in the monsoon season, disappear beneath a raging flood, but now it was just piled rocks as far as the eye could see. After lunch, I stepped into them for an ankle-wrenching walk.

Somewhere in the melée of rocks and boulders, the shape of one particular stone caught my eye and I went to investigate. It was rounded and pinkish, not very large, but it jutted out, smoother and with a different shine than the others around it. I bent down to pick it up, but it was caught fast by all the rocks around it and I could not shake it loose. Twice I gave up, and twice I returned to it—the second time getting it to shift slightly in its bed. My family was calling that it was time to leave, and I gave one last tug before turning away. Suddenly, it let go and released itself easily into my hands. That was what it felt like—that it *released* itself to me.

The stone was about ten inches tall and four inches wide, and extremely heavy—much heavier in heft than it looked. Perfectly rounded on top, it was flat at the base and looked like a lingam stone, a stylized phallic symbol representing the Hindu god Shiva that is found in temples throughout India and worshipped as a sign of generative power. Assuming that it was a natural river stone shaped intriguingly like a lingam, I claimed it as mine and took it home.

For years, I used this curious stone as a bookend, passing it every day on my way to the kitchen. Later, I brought it into service as a support for a portrait of my meditation teacher. I noticed one day that his face seemed to be moving, changing expression ever so slightly. I saw the hint of a smile and sensed that his eyes shifted, following me across the room when I stood up. I assumed it was my imagination, but for the next few days I observed his picture warily, watching for change. There it was—an extra glint in his eye, as if he were trying to tell me something. The sensation in my throat reminded me of Carnac.

I took down the picture and brought it and the stone outside to the light, where I could examine both more closely. My teacher's face expressed approval, it seemed to me, and on the stone—oh, my goodness—I saw for the first time a faint carved image of an encircling serpent. How had I missed that earlier? All this time I had assumed the stone to be a natural river rock shaped uncannily like a lingam, but it was not; it was an actual lingam!

Very likely, it had stood on the altar of a river temple through who knew how many wet and dry seasons? Perhaps it had been dislodged by raging waters during one year's flood, or perhaps it had lain in the riverbed for only a short time before I discovered it. I would never know.

By whatever fates, it had found its way to my home, and during the next decade it stood in the center of my altar, with the portrait of my teacher above it, and I bowed to them both daily. It stood there while our children grew up; it kept vigil while I was in Carnac. Then, one day many years later, after I had made contact with Natasha and Hamilton, I began to receive messages from it that felt similar to the ones I had received at the megaliths in Brittany.

I *heard* that I was to place the lingam again in living water as it had new work to do. My instructions were to build a fountain in my garden and place the lingam beneath a small waterfall, creating a new version of a river temple. I was asked to imagine a connection between my lingam and the standing stone on the mound in Kercado, to establish an energetic link between them.

I took the instructions seriously and when, after several months of hard work, the fountain was ready, I heard:

Place a crystal near the lingam to enhance its force. Do not buy one; it will come to you.

At first, I assumed I would find it on the ground somewhere, but after some months I forgot all about it. Then, one evening, I met a woman who asked out of the blue if I had an interest in stones.

"I'm a geologist," she explained with a grin, "and I always know another rock hound when I see one. Am I right?" I nodded, amazed. "Want to come see my collection?"

At her house, I was treated to one of the most fabulous assemblages of precious stones and crystals I had ever seen—large pieces of jade, smoky quartz, beryl, all over her house. She told me how she had come by each piece in the course of her career, and then she spoke of another collection bequeathed to her by her mentor when he died.

"Wait here," she said mysteriously. A while later, she returned with a massive aggregate of translucent white selenite that looked very much like a huge quartz crystal. It glinted gold in the light.

"I'm supposed to give this to you," she said quietly, telling me that her mentor, before he died, had charged her to distribute several stones in his collection to "the right person, when he or she comes along." She had given away three so far. This was the fourth.

Rather breathlessly, I told her the story of my fountain and the lingam, and that I was to wait for the fountain's crystal to come to me. For a few minutes we just smiled foolishly at one another. When I left her house, I carried the selenite crystal in my arms like a precious baby. It now sits alongside the fountain, next to the lingam, receiving spray and energy from the continuously flowing water and, I trust, doing whatever it is supposed to be doing.

My third stone came to me in a Mojave Desert canyon in Southern California, where my husband and I were hiking one spring. Shards of brownish sandstone flaked off the steep canyon walls, littering the ground in an area said to have fragile prehistoric sites that were deliberately unmarked to keep tourists away. It was our last day of hiking, and we stopped for lunch in a narrow, wild place where our voices echoed off the canyon walls and the hawks soared high above in a cloudless sky.

I sat amid the clinking shale, gazing about as I bit into my sandwich, and my eye fell upon an anomaly in the shale, a round gray rock with bumps on every surface. She (I immediately thought of the stone as "she") reminded me of the prehistoric Venus of Willendorf in Europe, a plump feminine figure with voluptuous curves suggesting belly and buttocks, head and shawl. The stone might well have been a natural shape enhanced by extra carving, and although it was small it was quite heavy to hold. I was sure I had found an ancient artifact that had once washed down during a flash flood from above.

The day was warm, but when I picked it up the stone felt cool in my palm. I was excited to have found what was clearly a treasure, and I would admire her before turning her in to the authorities at the trailhead. She fit perfectly into my fist, which I must have opened and closed a dozen times on the short walk out of the canyon, each time bonding with her a little bit more. At least until we found a park ranger, she would be mine. But although we went from office to office at the

The lingam stone and pool

visitors' center, nobody seemed to be concerned. I had found a rock, that's all. I did not argue—she was mine to keep.

That was more than twenty years ago, and ever since then she has been my "healing stone." She works with me, seated on the altar in my home studio, maintaining a high and steady vibration that I tune into before I do my healing work. I imagine she served a similar function long ago in the caves and ledges of another culture in the desert. I cannot imagine doing the work I do without her.

My next stone came to me some years later. I was with an aerial photographer on an adventure, scanning the Sonoran Desert in Arizona from above, flying low over the landscape in his two-seater as we searched out *intaglios*—large prehistoric designs that only make sense when seen from the air. We discovered several, some outlined by stones, some scratched into the hardpan of the desert floor, all depicting strange, stylized human and animal figures.

Our plan was to fly over one large serpent figure my friend had identified during an earlier flyby, land the plane at a small desert airport nearby, and drive back to examine it more closely. When we reached the approximate location by car, we used compass and intuition to find it again on the ground. At eye level, all that was visible of the creature was one long sine wave curve etched into hard sand.

I climbed a nearby rise to look down upon the design, marveling at its sinuous perfection. By my feet on the rounded ridge, I noticed an odd cluster of leathery brown stones, all polished to a sheen that gleamed in the desert sun. Other stones scattered about were shades of gray and white, as one might expect in this country.

The stone I picked up was as smooth as skin or polished leather and was pitted with minute holes. One by one, I lifted each of the shining brown stones, knowing I had made a remarkable find but not knowing, until I called my photographer friend over, just how remarkable. I had found the contents of a dinosaur's gizzard, he told me, which meant we were probably standing on dinosaur bones! He had had no idea that this was dinosaur country, and we wondered if that fact did not explain the serpent design sketched into the hardpan. We had made an extraordinary find! Reverently, I chose only one of the gizzard stones to take with me, a concave stone that fit into my palm perfectly.

I learned that scientists invariably found these clusters of polished stones at dinosaur digs, not understanding their significance for many years until they also observed that molar teeth had never been found among the animals' jawbones and teeth. Dinosaurs, they finally concluded, were ruminants and had apparently swallowed stones for grinding food in their gizzards, in the process polishing the stones to a hard sheen and leaving behind these clusters of leathery stone.

My brown stone served a long-gone being—a being whose very species is also long gone. It now serves as my meditation stone, helping me to ground myself every morning as I sit quietly with it tucked neatly in my palm. I especially like the poetic symmetry of using a grinding stone as a *grounding* stone!

I found my most recent stone—a jade harpoon point—on a beach in Northern California. I still do not know how it will be used. It sits with the gizzard stone and my little gray fossil stone on a shelf by my bed, and only when I feel a need for critical courage or insight do I reach for it. I do not think its purpose in my life has been revealed to me yet.

It was literally washed up at my feet by the surf, as I walked with friends on a long, sloping beach hours north of where I live. The sun was setting over the western ocean, and the pristine sands reflecting the orange ball of the sun were clear of seaweed wrack, our bare feet making prints that washed away with each new wave. My companions were walking ahead, when a new wave rushed in, dissolved into bubbles, and as it retreated left something on the sand that glinted green in the lowering light. I bent down to capture it before the next wave broke, finding in my hand a large jade arrowhead big enough to penetrate the pelt of an otter or seal. A lustrous green, shaped piece of jade.

Only years later, when a fire threatened our community, did I realize that I thought of my stones as "family." As the fire came closer and closer to our neighborhood, our family ran through the house salvaging what was most precious to each of us before our house went up in flames. I went first to the albums of family pictures, then ran to get my flute, while my husband went to his study for our legal papers and bank books. Our children each cleared their rooms of only the most precious of their belongings and, as billows of black smoke and red flames raced down the hills, I went to rescue my stones.

In the end, the fire was contained a few blocks from our neighborhood and our home was saved, but I had learned just how precious these stones were to me. I also realized, with a laugh at myself after the fire had been put out and life returned gradually to normal, that they were probably the only things in the house that would not have burned!

I remember reading once in an ancient Hindu text—*the Rig Veda*, I believe—a quatrain that went something like this:

> The Consciousness of the World sleeps in stone
> It breathes in plants
> It dreams in animals
> It awakens in humans.

This makes sense to me. If, indeed, the Universe itself is conscious, then everything that exists in it is also conscious—from the minute particles that make up matter, to rocks and all the plant and animal beings populating the Earth. And if everything is ultimately conscious, as I learned once at the stones in Carnac, then on some level everything is in communication with everything else. How could it be otherwise?

Since time immemorial people have called upon the supernatural powers of stones for healing and protection. Amulets, talismans, gemstones, and crystals have been used everywhere to ward off evil, to influence the Angels and preserve health. Magic stones, carved or rough, have sat upon altars in almost every culture of the world, receiving prayers and veneration and been worshipped as deities.

I have little doubt that my stones and I are in a similar kind of mysterious rapport. They have guided my hand more than once, responding to my prayers over the years, and I have had but to ask, knowing a flash of insight or synchronicity will occur before the day is out. I cannot help feeling that I am collaborating with these stones in a shared mission somehow, our work being about communicating Love in whatever ways we can.

What I experience, again and again, is gratitude for that bit of rock in my hand, on my fountain. Implicit within each of my stones are the fiery explosions of star-stuff that brought it into being; the long evolutions that formed its minerals; the ancient forces that shaped it into rock; the dinosaurs, then people, who changed or crafted it.

I share their history. I am connected to them by substance, evolution, and consciousness. By all of that—and more—we are relatives, my stones and I.

12

Natasha

And this our life, exempt from public haunt,
Finds tongues in trees, books in the running brooks,
Sermons in stones, and good in everything.
—WILLIAM SHAKESPEARE

Life in Stones

THE ELEMENTAL FORCES of our solar system power planet Earth, and those cosmic radiations affect our bodies and our daily lives in a multitude of ways. As our planet spins and travels around the sun, the fluctuating angles of sunlight and changing atmospheric conditions create regions of extreme heat or cold, and a more temperate climate in the areas between. Other cyclical happenings can bring to Earth the consciousness and subtle influence of the celestial spheres. Electrical storms carry lightning, or the element of Fire, into the soil to revitalize and regenerate it. The solar winds blow fiercely. Rain and snow are released from the atmosphere, sometimes destructively. When calm returns, the weather can be as gentle and pleasing to human life as a warm summer breeze.

Each of the elements—Fire, Air, Earth, and Water—stays in equilibrium with the others through their interlocking rhythms and cycles of change, their constant interplay being essential to keeping the planet alive. The ancient Greeks had an understanding of the effect of the elements on the human psyche; and Traditional Chinese Medicine explains the function of the main organs in the human body through their relationship with the seasons and the corresponding elemental influences.

The clear sparkling element of Water, which falls as rain or melting snow and ice from high mountain peaks, flows continuously over the crags and boulders that are the bones of the Earth, carrying fragments of the great mountain ranges, tumbling them downstream and polishing them, through the continuous pounding of water over the millennia, into smaller rocks and pebbles.

Spilling down the mountainside, the streams meander, ever widening until they become a river en route to the ocean, where it finally slows and spreads itself over the soft sands of the seashore. There it eddies and plays with seashells, bearing the messages from the mountain air that have accompanied its pebbles and water.

Not all stone is worn away in this manner. Much rock laid down under the sea over past millennia, and thrown up in volcanic upheavals and hardened at the surface, is easily accessible. It was put to use by past generations of mankind as the megaliths we can still see today.

Those massive constructions, especially the long rows of standing stones at Carnac, can generate local energy from the dance of earthly and cosmic forces upon them. This is akin to a low-frequency electrical field, resulting from the interaction of quartz and mica particles in the structure of stone caused by heat or pressure. The Carnac groupings made use of crystalline granite, not only because it was locally available but also because it could hold the input of energy from the sun.

Two menhirs, Ste.-Barbe

We can say that the whole area of Carnac is alive in an electrical sense; fueled by the elements, it is an excellent "plugging-in" spot, a good place to recharge our spiritual and physical batteries. Many of the more remote sacred places on the planet have a similar function, but their power is sometimes too extreme for such human interaction. Carnac, however, seems to have been designed for just this purpose. It is a place where the elemental forces are filtered in subtle ways, making the interconnection of Spirit and Matter more easily accessible to human consciousness.

Brittany, and especially Carnac, was chosen for this by the elemental beings because the power generated in the stone rows enables the voices of those Angelic messengers to be held there, silently captured in the stone itself, until activated by interaction with the human mind. Each stone, and each row of stones, carries a polarity that alternates with its neighbor; they are bound together in alternating currents of positive and negative energies, vibrations that have been programmed to hold information. The positive and negative energies of these fields do not represent good and bad, in the sense those words are often used in our language; rather, they indicate that one is active and the other receptive, in a back-and-forth movement that seeks equilibrium. Those balancing qualities are inherent in all life.

Electricity is not a modern invention; it is more accurate to say we have "discovered" a force that has always existed as a binding element in matter. The electrical energy fields of humans, animals, plants, and minerals are enhanced through their association with each other, and in the case of stone and crystal, can carry memory and information just as water does.*

Those mineral elements can both transmit and receive, and so may be used for a variety of communication purposes, whether conscious or not. They can work closely with the energies of the human heart chakra, or energy center, and when programmed with heartfelt, loving intention, they can serve to amplify thoughts of protection and healing. However, human beings must reach a certain level of self-empowerment and integrity before working with stones and crystals in this way, to avoid ceding their own power to the mineral kingdom, or in other ways to misuse its potential.

The mineral kingdom is not "dead matter": it has its own sphere of influence and is a force to be treated with respect. As an integral participant in the life of the planet, it has a link with cosmic forces. That is inherent in us all, but often we forget that each one of us is also part of a greater whole and need to be reminded of it.

---

* See *Love Thyself: The Message from Water III* by Masaru Emoto (Carlsbad, CA: Hay House, 2006)

Crystal carries the rainbow prism of light in its structure, and as such it carries the clarity of the Creator's blueprint for life. This etheric blueprint has the ability to restore life to its perfect harmonic vibration as it reaches into the energy field of an individual person or animal. This means that crystals and stones, when intentionally programmed with the vibrations of sound or thought, can help to maintain balance and harmony in both the human body and the environment. Some healers program crystals with a musical note to resonate specifically with the person they are treating, bringing them to a state of equilibrium by harmonizing with the vibrational field of their aura.

As crystals hold pure vibrations of light, an important part of the electromagnetic spectrum, they may also be used to shield places in the landscape or people's homes from inharmonious or damaging influences. Being in harmony with the life force, itself an expression of Light, crystals can be used to restore harmony where it is found to be lacking.

The crystal, as is true of much of the mineral kingdom, embodies an intrinsic will to cooperate. To regard crystals merely as decorative objects is to ignore their level of awareness. That is a loss to human development, as they are increasingly a part of our modern life, many being artificially produced as resonating memory chips for computer technology. All of them have the potential to interact with human intelligence. It seems to be part of the mineral kingdom's evolution to do so, as well as being essential to the advancement of our own.

As our ability to work in cooperation with various forms of crystals, gemstones, and minerals is enhanced, so will our understanding of the physical world develop, many times in what may appear extraordinary ways. Nutritionists know that within the physical body there are tiny but essential levels of minerals—the so-called trace elements that work to maintain our physical bodies in optimum health. When one is lacking, we become ill.

Similarly, the crystals and minerals within the body of the Earth help to maintain the health of the planet; they are not there simply to be plundered. The Earth itself suffers when crystals and minerals are taken from wherever they belong. Hidden within their crystal caves, they work to create a vital resonance and harmony, as though resonating in an underground cathedral; if we could hear them, we would know they were singing to the Earth, mother of us all.

Once in a while, the mineral kingdom lets us find certain stones when we need them, and occasionally they speak to us. That was what happened to us when we received messages from the great stones of Carnac and were able to write about their meaning for us. If respect were given to these living guardians of the Light, and their permission sought before they were cut from the living rock, our interaction with the mineral kingdom would be one of true and beneficial cooperation.

The human soul can be viewed as a many-faceted crystal, each facet representing an opportunity for the soul to experience and grow. After many incarnations, the various facets may become more highly polished, ever more able to reflect the light of the Creator, and only then may the individual soul return to the Source and become one with the Light. In the Biblical Book of Revelations, gemstones and crystals symbolically form the foundation of the New Jerusalem; and in the Book of Exodus, the high priest Aaron is described as wearing gemstones in his breastplate, each one signifying a particular quality of importance for humankind.

Stone and crystal retain an affinity with the collective qualities of the elemental group consciousness from which they were formed. Like all other forms, they are not separate but part of the whole, just as human beings are part of a larger, collective field of consciousness, even when as individuals we appear to be isolated from each other.

Some of the megaliths of Carnac in Brittany—as well as many others elsewhere—have repetitive patterns engraved upon them whose meanings are still mysterious, even to scholars. Although strange, they are also disturbingly familiar, rather like the geometric patterns in crop circles, as if we know just what they mean but cannot quite remember. Often they can be found inside dolmens, on stones encircling a mound, in the passageway or on a blocking stone deep within an inner chamber, where they would have been hidden from the sight of all but the initiates.

The fine engravings found on standing stones and rocky outcrops worldwide; the magnificent, even older paintings within the caves of Lascaux in France, Altamira in Spain, in Brazil and elsewhere—all these various markings had different functions according to their makers' purpose. Some probably activated the energy required for certain rites of passage, or enhanced the shamans' ability to commune with unseen forces. Some may have assisted the departing souls of the dead to return to their cosmic origins, and others may have served as wayside markers to the sacred places. Certain patterns can be activated by tracing the design with the hand or eye, or by dancing around the larger stones. Such conscious interaction has the ability to bring sleeping stones to life, as they then register an increase in the strength of their alternately charged energy fields.

The ideas and information represented by abstract symbols have always had a place in the development of human history. Shapes take on a power of their own that increases when we understand what they stand for. As meaningful symbols, they engage us to respond, emotionally and instinctively. Today's advertising logos are an example of this kind of communication: we see a simple design and get the reference immediately, whether perfume, food, or even a handbag!

Seashell and pebbles

Other patterns have symbolic power, but since they apparently exist only in the ether, they remain hidden until found by dowsing or inner sensing. For instance, the medieval Knights Templar were able to imprint the ground at their *commanderies* with mystic symbols, often a cross, seemingly by a process of thought combined with the power of intention.

Encircling every church built on an old pagan site, and around certain menhirs, there can be found a dowsable ring of protective energy dating back to prehistoric times. Where the Athene and Apollo energy lines (twin currents described in an earlier chapter) cross to form a nodal point, it is possible to dowse a flowerlike pattern that expands and becomes more regular in shape in response to that human recognition.

It may be that such elegant patterns, ethereally imprinted in the ground or engraved on standing stones, embody the essence of the cosmic forces that created and continue to maintain our planet Earth. With the power to activate the fundamental elements of which all things are formed, such patterns enable us to develop a greater affinity with all that is, because *we* are part of all that is.

And when an intriguing stone, shell, or crystal comes our way, perhaps we are being given a nudge and a chance, metaphorically, to "hold hands with the Universe."

13

Carolyn

Synchronicity

IT WAS CARL JUNG who first coined the word "synchronicity," writing:

> Telepathy, clairvoyance, and precognition are all synchronicities—meaningful coincidences between persons and events in which an emotional or symbolic connection cannot be explained by cause and effect.

He went on to say that what we in the West considered to be random chance, the ancient Chinese presumed to be a significant confluence of events, and therefore meaningful for their lives.

From time to time, I had experienced these odd coincidences, but it was not until I read Jung's statement and had the following strange occurrence that I started paying attention to the synchronicities in my life.

One evening, washing up the supper dishes, I found myself thinking about a friend from my student days in France—another Carolyn. We had been called *les deux Carolines*, both adventurous American girls hitchhiking around the countryside and having a wonderful time. That had been years ago, though, and we had since lost contact. The last time we had seen each other was in New York, just before I married and moved across the country. Since then, only the occasional bit of news, then years of nothing.

The next day she phoned! My jaw dropped. She had just flown into San Francisco, she said, and could not get me out of her mind during the whole plane ride. When they landed, she took a chance and looked me up in the local phone book under my married name.

"And here you are!" she exclaimed, gleefully. Our reunion was, of course, joyous; especially when we discovered that the friends she was visiting had the same names as the members of my family, so that when we all got together there were two Carolyns, two Rebeccas, and two Herbs.

I think this kind of thing happens to most of us: we think of somebody and hear from them shortly thereafter; we are late and meet the love of our life on the next train; we read an unusual word, then it keeps popping up everywhere we look. More often than not, the chance happening is just what we needed at that moment—the right person, the new idea, the fortuitous encounter. A good example of this was finding Natasha and Hamilton's well-known first book *Let The Standing Stones Speak* at a bookstore on the other side of town that I had felt compelled to visit.

I had a manuscript to photocopy that day. Normally, I walk to our neighborhood photocopy center, but on that day I *knew* I had to drive all the way across town to a copy center where I could browse in a nearby bookstore while I waited. I recall feeling anticipation as I approached the bookstore, and as I entered, there it was, right in front of me—Natasha and Hamilton's book. Had I not obeyed that inner urge to do things differently that day, we would never have known about each other and *Voices Out of Stone* would never have been written.

Sometimes coincidences are not that straightforward but involve people and events occurring over time, and sometimes space. For me, such coincidences often seem to involve flutes.

Years ago, I received an ebony flute that had been thrown out as trash by someone cleaning out the flotsam and jetsam of her late grandfather's attic. It was passed on to me by a friend who had rescued it from the pile, and for many years I played this priceless treasure with great delight. Eventually, though, my musical interests turned toward improvisational singing and I played my flute less and less, eventually putting it in a drawer. Sadly, it sat there for a long time gathering dust.

Then, one day, a series of synchronicities began to occur. They started when I bumped into a woman I had known thirty years earlier, when her brother and I had been engaged. She lived several hours away and happened to be visiting town that day. Shortly before her brother's recent death, he had phoned me to say a final goodbye, thanking me for our time together and saying that his life had never quite made sense after our parting. I doubted that I was the primary cause of his unhappiness, but still I felt deeply saddened and wished I knew how to clear the hurt between us. Then came one coincidence after another.

My husband and I received an invitation not only to the same city this woman lived in, but on the same street! Phoning her to suggest we come by when we were there, I caught her at the very moment she had returned to the house to retrieve something she had forgotten.

When we drove up her street a few days later, we heard the tones of a flute being practiced, wafting out of an upstairs window—hers, as it turned out. The flutist was her daughter, niece of my former fiancé. A serious musician, she was as in love with the flute as I had once been, and by that evening I knew where my precious ebony flute was to go. She was as astonished to receive the unexpected gift of this remarkable instrument as I had been to have it come into my life those many years earlier, and it created a bond of trust that had once been broken between her uncle's family and me. After all, under different circumstances I might have been her aunt—and I feel the chasm of hurt between him and me is finally healed.

Over time, I have noticed that projects that heal or benefit others in some way tend to call up these helpful coincidences. I often wonder if the Universe itself isn't encouraging my better efforts—those times when I can let go of expectations and simply trust. I am often awed by what comes marching in the door.

As someone fascinated by the interface between science and spirit, I mostly have to break trail in little-charted territory, and often I come to a crossroads, not knowing how to proceed.

At one such stopping point, I received a call from a stranger who had heard about my work and wished to come for a session. We worked together for a few hours, and as he left he handed me a sheaf of papers. They sat on my "to read" pile until I brought them along for airplane reading when I went to visit one of my children. One article happened to be from a research institute in the city my kids lived in, so I decided to pay the institute a visit.

My meeting with the people there was warm and friendly and resulted in a enthusiastic exchange of books, ideas and promises of mutual assistance. They circulated my work to some of the most seminal, cutting edge thinkers in the world today, and the result has been collaborations and friendships that continue to inform my life and work every day. I cannot imagine where I would be without that fortuitous meeting.

Jung writes:

> The understanding of synchronicity is the key which unlocks the door to the Eastern apperception of totality that we find so mysterious.

The ancient Chinese oracle, the *I Ching,* or Book of Changes, is based upon the belief that the material world as we know it is a reflection of an underlying reality in which all things are connected and in the process of continuous transformation. Nothing ever stays the same; everything in the Cosmos is perpetually in motion, every particle shifting in relation to every other particle, everything synchronized in time and space.

Musically speaking, it as though every chord, each tone of every movement in a Universal Symphony is playing simultaneously, harmonizing everything, everywhere, at this very moment. All things are interrelated, interdependent, interpenetrating. Nothing is excluded—from shimmering subatomic particles to swirling galaxies.

Now... becomes now... becomes now...

According to Jung, the world has an underlying order, a "collective unconscious," a shared memory in which all beings are bonded by deep patterns that connect us to each other and to the Cosmos. In such a Universe, synchronicities are literally "co-incidences"—simultaneously occurring events in which their meaning or significance is immediately apparent to the person experiencing them.

When I began paying attention to these coincidences in my own life, I tried to take a scientific approach to the matter. I kept careful notes to determine if there was a pattern to these coincidences, and I looked for correlations between what I was doing when they tended to happen. I noted the weather, the time of year, the phase of the moon, my menses, my emotions, and how my body felt when the coincidences occurred.

Here is what I discovered.

When I was busy and around a lot of people, I rarely noticed synchronicities; however, when I was more contemplative and spent time alone, they were more evident. When I was engaged in creative work and, therefore receptive to subtle signals, I was frequently aware of synchronicities: the more sensitive my emotional state, the more I noticed myself experiencing synchronicities. When I was angry, preoccupied, jealous, or self-righteous, I rarely experienced them. The biggest surprise was to note that extreme weather conditions, especially storms with thunder and lightening, seemed to bring forth synchronicities by the dozens.

For example, right now as I write these words in the winter of 2008, we have had a series of rainstorms with occasional thunder and lightning, which is rare in our part of California, and coincidences seem to be coming thick and fast. Just this past week I received a call from someone who makes greenhouses, exactly when I was reading about how to make a greenhouse for the garden. The best coincidence of the week, however, was meeting a neighbor at the library, where I was searching for a particular, out-of-print book, only to learn that she was the author's daughter and had the book at home!

So how might we understand what is going on here? To find answers, I became a hunter-gatherer, stalking diverse subjects from Hermetic philosophy and ancient Chinese divination to fractal geometry and chaos theory. In a nutshell, what I found is that mystical traditions the world over describe the Universe as a whole, interrelated system in time and space in which all parts, visible and invisible, are connected to every other part. The sacred and the everyday intersect and everything is in communion with everything else. In these traditions, contemplation of the whole is an ecstatic experience, and profound gratitude to be alive in the world is the result.

Contemporary science, although based on the understanding of the world as three-dimensional rather than multidimensional, also now posits that there is an inherent roughness to the world, a kind of wild diversity that is constantly changing on every scale. Science has begun to recognize that even as all things are vibrating with wild abandon, they are in constant communication with each other, and on the level of the whole there is an overall, interpenetrating order. This mysterious background "something" is called dark matter, dark energy. Gradually, science is coming to recognize that, at the deepest level, still elusive to our most sophisticated instruments, there seems to be something like a spirit of cooperation, an inherent awareness in our world—in a word, a consciousness.

Until now in our culture, we have been taught that reality is linear, that objects are separate from one another, that "proof" requires the repetition of the same reaction again and again. But we are learning that the boundaries isolating one thing from another exist only at the most superficial levels, like bubbles at the surface of the stew-pot, and the more closely we look, the more clearly we see that everything is happening at once, bouncing and bumping off everything else, all arising from the common brew. An impulse originating right here, right now, can have unforeseen consequences elsewhere in the world—at this moment or far into the future; and perhaps the past, as well. In fact, the mutual interdependence of everything with everything is such that even an imperceptible shift may have ramifications for every level of the Cosmos, for all time. In these treacherous times, I find this encouraging.

To me it would be surprising if, in such a world, synchronicities did *not* occur!

If the theory in quantum physics of "nonlocality" is correct—the fact that two photons or electrons, wherever they are or how far apart, are responsive to each other, directly and instantaneously without need of any mechanical intermediary—then it would follow that our thoughts and intentions are capable of the same immediate connection with the thoughts of others. The ability to receive the thoughts and feelings of others, or to transmit our own, either consciously or unconsciously, ought to be possible by definition, if, as I believe to be the case, our world is composed of more than just what we humans can see, hear, and measure. We could be capable of a lot more than we have been taught to suppose. It is upon this premise that I base my understanding of this phenomenon we call Synchronicity.

From my experiences in Brittany, and refined over the years, I have come to recognize a certain quality of feeling in my mind and body when I am "in the zone." I can *feel* when I should go ahead with a plan and count on these helpful surprises. I can sense a kind of internal quietude or relaxed ease, a feeling of being located right in the center of myself. It is a sense of belonging where I am—in the right place at the right time—a knowing that I can trust myself. Worry, doubt, and uncertainty seem irrelevant, and in the way. Somehow, I have faith that the pieces will come together in ways I cannot anticipate, but if I relax and give myself over to the pleasure of the moment, the results will be pleasing to me. The "pleasure" part is particularly important!

Conversely, if I plan too much in advance and strain to make something happen out of anxiety, it will often go badly and have to be done all over again.

I once worked with a hunger organization. A caterer donated a commercial refrigerator to us, free of charge, if we would move it. We didn't need a refrigerator, but we badly needed a freezer. However, after much discussion, we decided to accept. The first attempt to move it failed because the truck broke down; the next time, our helpers had the wrong date. When we finally got a truck and helpers together, the door the refrigerator had to go through wasn't wide enough. Finally, with thanks and apologies, we gave up. Two days later an anonymous caller donated a freezer, delivery included.

Sometimes a single, fortuitous coincidence prepares the way for the next opportunity, which then leads to yet another remarkable coincidence—all unpredictable and often involving people and events far removed from each other in time and space. At such times, we may feel that a ministering Angel is in charge, or that we are being used as agents for a set of circumstances much larger than anything we might imagine.

Here is another flute story. While traveling in India in the 1960s, I met a remarkable musician who played the North Indian bass flute. He wished to bring his music to the burgeoning world-music scene in America, and I promised to deliver a demonstration tape to people I knew in California. (This was long before CDs or computers or IPods.) When I got home, I was distracted with many other things, and the tape lay at the bottom of a pile for eighteen months. Then one day I awoke knowing that this was the day, and I phoned our local public radio station to tell them about my tape.

"What a coincidence!" the program director exclaimed. "We have a crisis here because our 11 a.m. show has canceled, and we've been scrambling to find a substitute. Can you come right down?" Of course I could! On the air I played the music, telling the musician's story, and saying that he was looking to play in America.

The radio show was heard—coincidentally, of course—by someone from a local College of North Indian music who, as it happened, was trying to find a teacher of North Indian flute.

"I never listen to the radio at that time!" he told me. "It was pure accident that I turned on that program just when he was playing!" The rest, of course, is history.

I have often wondered why it took me so long to follow through on my promise to this musician; what made that person turn on his radio that morning; why my path crossed with the musician's in the first place?

It was as if we were all tuned to the same frequency of intention without knowing it, and thus made this fortuitous contact at the perfect moment. Like several waves cresting simultaneously on the same sea, we were bonded by the medium of our shared ocean. Unknown to each other, we each responded to a similar impulse and, like secret agents working undercover on a larger mission, we collectively created the conditions that brought this musician to America, thereby giving him his opportunity to play for a worldwide audience, and us years of delight in hearing his music.

For me, synchronicities feel akin to falling in love. Every time one happens, I get a glimpse of the ecstatic fabric of the Universe, the miracle and the simplicity, the ordered Wholeness and the wild shimmying of its exuberant dance. Every time, I learn a little bit more about how to tune in and relax, accepting it as a gift received—a penny from Heaven. I find that the more I accept synchronicities as real, the more they tend to happen. The more they happen, the more faith I have that they will happen again. Without the resistance of disbelief, things fall into place with little effort on my part. Synchronicities have become one of the ordinary miracles of my everyday life.

Years ago, while on a bicycle trip through Ireland, I found myself at Trinity College in Dublin, where the sixth-century illuminated manuscript *The Book of Kells* is on display in a hermetically sealed glass case, opened each day to a single page. The manuscript is ancient and vulnerable and is taken out only in very special circumstances. Since I have a special love for medieval art, I returned to the college library for three days in a row to examine that day's page. On the fourth day, I impulsively decided to knock on the door of the office and simply ask if there were any way I might see the whole manuscript. It was a rash and even irrational act on my part, but something propelled me toward that door.

Unbelievably, at the secretary's desk sat a friend from my student days, when we studied medieval art history together in France! She is the only native Irish person I have ever known well, and I had not seen her in years. She might also be one of the few people in existence who would know of my serious interest in the Middle Ages! After our mutual delight at finding one another again, she intervened on my behalf and I was granted the rare permission to examine the whole Book of Kells the next morning.

Magic abounds—the subtle signals are available for all of us to hear. It is a matter of learning how to listen to what is there, just beneath our sense of hearing but within reach of our felt senses. For me, when it is working, I can feel a resonance, a being in tune, a rightness. If the Universe is singing all the time, my guess is that we can all tune into it at will and feel for the rhythm, breathe with the music, and start dancing!

Crop Circles

IN THE PEAK OF SUMMER, in the early 1990s, while getting ready to board a bus in Cornwall, a county in the extreme southwest of England, a newspaper headline at the newsagent's stand caught my eye: "Strange Formations Appear in Wiltshire Wheat Field." An aerial photograph showed a complex pictogram of ringed circles in a row, sprouting lines and fingers—an ancient rune in wheat. I boarded the bus. My destination, as it happened, was the county of Wiltshire.

This was not the first time I had heard about crop circles. Since the 1970s I had been following stories of unexplained circles showing up—overnight, in most cases—in English fields of oats, wheat, barley, and oilseed rape. Mostly, they were being reported in the West Country, in the area surrounding the prehistoric sites of Stonehenge and Avebury. I suspected there might be a connection with the megaliths there, but I had no idea what and was glad to have the chance to feel it out for myself. Since I was on my way to Wiltshire to meet the grand lady of Earth mysteries, Mary Scott, I would have the good fortune to explore with her this very formation in the neighboring Vale of Pewsey.

As it happened, this crop circle was the first in a series of complex designs that would appear not only in England but all over the world. As I write, in 2008, they are still appearing. Since the first sighting of a swirled, simple circle in a farmer's field almost forty years ago, the circles have increased in numbers and design elements: sometimes many circles appeared together in lines, crosses, or spirals; sometimes the lay of the grain was counter-clockwise, sometimes several circles were connected by rings, or surrounded by concentric circles.

But this pictogram at Alton Barnes, in the Vale of Pewsey, took a leap of imagination and galloped for eighty meters across a field of wheat, sporting seven circles of varying sizes, some ringed and others with extra arms and fingers. It was so enormous it could only be seen in its entirety from the air, and until we walked into it, all we could see from the roadside were subtle indentations in the ripening crop. The farmers were as puzzled as those of us who had shown up at their farm in the middle of the week. They asked for a pound to enter their fields and exchanged exclamations and information with us when we eventually came out, mystified.

The farmers claimed the pictogram had not been there when they had left the fields at dusk, but it was there in all its glory the next morning at dawn. It seemed impossible, we all agreed, that people could have come in during the night and, in pitch darkness, produced a design of such complex perfection without even rousing the local dogs to barking! The farmers claimed they found the rest of the field untrampled, the dew unbroken, with no sign of footprints or cigarette butts or the remains of a sandwich. No sweaters had been left behind, no broken stalks in the tractor tramlines, nothing whatsoever to indicate that anyone had been there in the night except for this massive work of art in which stalks had been bent but not broken, in which the wheat appeared to be continuing to grow, in which every edge in the design was crisp and perfect.

When Mary and I walked in, we went first to the farthest end of one "finger," where the design rick-racked intricately into smaller and smaller Vs. In the final series of Vs, we counted exactly nine stalks of wheat laid down in each one. Nine. Mary, who was almost eighty years old at the time, was initially quite sceptical about the phenomenon, although Earth mysteries had been her field for more than half a century. But when we discovered those nine stalks in each V, she looked up at me with astonished eyes, and even though the day was hot, we both shivered.

Throughout the following decade, pictograms by the hundreds were reported all over the world: in blueberries and corn, sunflowers and snow—even in trees in Czechoslovakia! The formations became larger and more complex and, day by day, the circle-makers—whoever or whatever they were—seemed to be perfecting their art. Strange new and intricate geometries appeared in the designs. Photographs showed woven stalks that caught the changing light, giving the impression of three-dimensionality and multiple textures. Grain was tufted, laid in different directions, nested. As the seasons and years wore on, the designs became more intricate, more playful, and more beautiful than those before.

Meanwhile, unless you lived near the fields themselves or faithfully logged onto the few Web sites reporting on the phenomenon, you would think it wasn't happening at all. The media stayed mum; that is, until two jocular fellows in their sixties claimed to have dreamed up the game in the pub one evening and had done it as a lark. At last, there was something to report: *it had all been a hoax.* After years of silence on the subject of crop circles, the "hoax" made the evening television news in California!

The fact that these two men had no way of explaining how they managed to complete several crop circles every night in different parts of England, not to mention elsewhere in the world, was never discussed. When threatened suit by the farmers whose crop had been lost, they confessed they had only done a few, but by that time the media was no longer watching. A demonstration of their craft resulted in a clumsy mess, but that was later and not reported in the mainstream press. And when extraordinary designs continued to appear, even after one of the men had died—they were, after all, getting a bit old for all that running around—

most everybody seemed to have lost interest. Even now, when the subject comes up informally at a party somebody will ask, "Didn't two guys do it?"

In fact, in the past decade or so, people *have* tried their hands at it, and some have been remarkably adept at creating impressive formations in the fields. Personally, I find this a fascinating development and a testament to human imagination and will. But if just *one* out of the thousands of formations that have appeared all over the world in the last forty years was not made by humans, the mystery still exists and deserves attention. And if hundreds of people all over the world have been creating them all along, expending such energy, imagination, and artistry so discreetly without need for recognition or recompense, I'd say that was at least as extraordinary as if it were done by some mysterious agency.

It is the resistance on the part of the mainstream culture to giving this phenomenon the attention it deserves that interests me here.

A few years ago, a friend called late at night to say he had just learned that a crop circle had touched down in a wheat field about an hour's drive from our home in California. Imagine that! At dawn, we whisked some unsuspecting house-guests out of bed and went to have a look. As soon as the car was parked, I streaked out and entered the first circle of an enormous formation.

Everything about the circle reminded me of the atmosphere at Alton Barnes: ripening grain swirled into golden circles, above which the air felt sweet, a formation so large and complex we could not decipher it from the ground. Only a few people had arrived that early, and in the morning quiet we greeted each other with soft smiles, walking from one circle to the next, following the connecting pathways and exploring the outermost rings.

As was the case in England, the design was on too large a scale to read from the ground and, just as in England, it seemed to have no end, one circle connecting to the next, the wheat swirling clockwise in some places, counter-clockwise in others, the stalks bent but not broken, the edges crisp. Later, comparing photographs taken in both places, I could not easily tell which was which.

When a team of journalists arrived, I was glad to tell them what I knew from my experience in England. They also interviewed the others making their way around the formation, as well as the farmer. The next morning, there I was on the front page of the newspaper, my words twisted in a derisive article about New Age gullibility. We had all been duped, the article proclaimed, as four teenagers had given them the "real" story about the prank they had played that night in the field.

The farmer, however, who had never heard of crop circles before this, was not so easily convinced. He was impressed by the reverence of the crowds who continued to show up at his farm, could feel something unusual in the air when he entered his

fields and, knowing the boys personally, did not believe them to be capable of creating anything of such perfection and beauty. He gave them a challenge: he would sacrifice another half-acre of his wheat-fields to them to demonstrate to the community and the newspaper reporters how they had done the job, to prove that it was their work. They refused, finally confessing they had not done the deed but had been paid to pretend they had. I never did find out by whom.

By the time the teens confessed, nobody was paying attention any longer, and when the newspaper finally covered the revised story, it was a short squib on the back page. A week later, another beautiful formation showed up in a field nearby. This time the media ignored it altogether.

For years I have wondered why there is so much resistance to the possibilities of unexplained phenomena, to the idea that there might be more dimensions to our world than we are aware of. Many people I know, particularly scientists, tend to be adamant, even hostile, toward what they refer to as my "nonstandard" view of the world.

Recently, I got a hint of why this resistance was so entrenched, during an evening I spent with some astronomer friends. Somebody told the story of an oddball colleague whose ideas were considered unacceptable enough that, while he was given an office, he was allowed neither to teach nor to publish. Curious, I asked them the nature of this colleague's ideas. From their description, his ideas sounded a bit extreme but otherwise reasonable to me, so I asked why they had such an excessive reaction to him. I was laughingly told that if it should it turn out he was right, they would all have to scrap everything they knew and start again from scratch.

Bingo! There it was—the ring of truth. We would, indeed, have to rethink everything we presume to be true, and start from scratch if our culture were to accept the following: the Universe is composed of interpenetrating dimensions that include, but are not limited to, the three-dimensional world; all systems are connected, visible and invisible, to all other systems; Time and Space exist within No-Time and No-Space. If I had been brought up on the scientific method, I would find this daunting, too.

But perhaps we have no choice. When I gaze at aerial photographs of crop circles that continue to appear year after year, what I see is whole systems in which every part is related to every other part, the whole forming a thing of beauty. Like us, the parts do not exist independently of the whole; instead, they participate in a sacred Wholeness that includes not only the material world that we can see, touch, hear, and measure but also the vast Everything—dark and light, good and evil, seen and unseen. In this Wholeness, everything is interconnected and in constant flux, and nothing is outside the Whole. To me, it is a wonder of such proportions, so right and inclusive, that I cannot understand why anybody, given a choice, would consider anything less.

It seems significant that crop circles are appearing primarily in grain, the staff of life. Consider this: in the staple food crops of every corner of the globe—wheat, corn, oats, barley, rice, soybean, millet—wherever these mysterious designs appear, the grain has been discovered to have enhanced nutritive value. What are we to make of this?

Hunger is rampant in the world, our societies know little about sharing, and the situation is getting worse. Children starve and sicken while nations stockpile food until it rots. As a species we seem to have lost our way, scrambling blindly on an increasingly more violent road, fouling the nest of the Earth, starving and murdering our siblings and neglecting our young. It is as if we have forgotten why we are here.

We are out of balance now. The center is barely holding. Great changes are imminent and, if we are to survive, it seems to me that we've got to make a big shift in our thinking—soon. If our astronomers are searching the sky for intelligent life elsewhere in the Universe, might it not also be the case that Intelligence of some unknown form is trying to reach us as well?

And if so, could we not ask for a more brilliant, beautiful, playful way for it to happen than crop circles, an artform that even inspires some of us to try and imitate it? A living artform that recycles every year, does not despoil the Earth but feeds people, mulches the soil, fascinates, and teaches us? To me, crop circles are the biggest news in town, bigger than all the wars and politics of the whole planet put together. Each year's formations are knockouts. Check them out on the Internet. You'll love them.

14

Carolyn

My Garden

DECADES AFTER MY TIME IN BRITTANY, following my mother's death I decided to transform our front lawn of thick crabgrass beneath a sprawling incense cedar tree into a garden. It was my personal grieving ritual and particularly apt, as clearing the mat of tangled crabgrass would be like clearing tangled emotions. It was just what I needed right then—to tear out the tenacious weeds that ran for yards deep in the ground, just like in my heart.

I started by randomly pulling at the scraggly stuff. For at least a week, I gathered huge piles of knobbly green grass and tossed it into the city compost bins, but once I got down to the hard clay, the clearing work really began. I watered the bare dirt to soften it, then, using a pitchfork, trowel, and hoe, dug down for the runners. The deeper I penetrated the ground, the deeper went the roots. A job I had thought would take a week or so was going to take me much longer—months, perhaps. Each tenacious runner would have to be extricated by hand, one by one, and with each runner a strand of sadness in my heart would get pulled up as well. Crabgrass can propagate by even one small fragment of a root, so the soil would have to be sifted for strays as well. Taking on this job might be more than I had bargained, but then, so was my mother.

She had given birth to me at the age of eighteen, on the run from a tragic family of her own, with neither the inclination nor the ability to mother a child. She was a gifted and wilful teenager during the Second World War, who longed to be a musician but married out of desperation. I arrived soon after. When her beloved brother died in the war, my mother became paralyzed and snapped, losing her grip on reality. For as long as I could remember she retreated inside her disappointed dreams, surviving in confusion and rage until the age of almost ninety.

With only a tick of hesitation, I took on the crabgrass caper. It was now or never. By the end of the first day, with only one small patch cleared, I felt that my mother and I were finally talking. And we were, but the conversation with her was through *the* Mother—Mother Earth.

By the second week, the satisfaction of following a deep runner back to its root source was profound, as if I was clearing out yet another choking constriction from my own ground. I could feel in my body where to dig next in the dirt, and first thing the next morning I would put my pitchfork in that spot and dig there. Weeding my garden was like weeding myself.

People passing by, seeing me out there day after day, began to stop and chat. What was I doing there sitting in the dirt, pulling away at weeds with such concentration? To some, I just said I was making a garden; to others, I told the larger truth, and several of those people responded by telling me their own stories of loss. When that happened, I stopped work and listened. One woman, whose husband had recently died, was so distraught I invited her in for tea, and we cried together. One man, remembering boyhood days working on his mother's farm in Louisiana, stooped down and pulled weeds with me. Even before this garden had a single plant, or even the loam to plant it in, I found that I was making a healing garden.

Having cleared the ground down to about two feet, and along with it much of my own long-held grief, it was time to let in the light. The incense cedar, with its huge crown of gnarly branches spreading in all directions, completely shaded the yard and much of the street. Cutting it down was out of the question—it had been my precious bit of wildness in the city for too long—but I would consider thinning it, especially after being assured that a pruning would make the tree stronger.

Three agile men climbed into its branches and, in less than four hours much of the tree was on the ground, curved and sculpted limbs littering every inch of bare soil. The spaces now visible in its crown opened like wide windows letting in the light of the sun more, then still more.

Neighbors and passersby were on hand to witness the transformation. Among them was Pete, a woodworker, who gazed covetously at the branches on the ground.

"Oh, gorgeous!" he kept saying as each curvaceous limb hit the earth with a thunk. "That would make a fabulous back for a chair… a bedpost…" Both of us, I think, got the idea at the same time and, catching each other's eye, laughed in recognition.

A fence! An arbor! A bower! A trellis! Benches! Here? Yes, and there! How?

"I know how," he said.

"Would you help me?" I said, making hand sketches in the air.

"With pleasure," he said. The creative urge gathered us up like a wave cresting

The Garden Arbor

in the sea, and we shook hands excitedly, agreeing to meet "at the garden" the next morning to work it all out.

That night, working by the light of a moon whose glow shone right through the open branches, I was out there by myself stacking wood, placing the narrow pieces in the first pile, the middle-girth limbs next, and the heaviest ones over to the side. Alone in the dark, I imagined a gateway with its arbor, a bower by the chimney, the trellis in the corner, and roses a-bloom everywhere! I could hardly wait until morning.

According to the principles of permaculture—a technique of land use and restoration for bringing health back to wasted land—everything on the land can be recycled, used in a new way. Nature wastes nothing, and therefore neither should we. By being creative with the elements at hand, we may take a wasteland and turn it into an Eden.

Pete and I got to it the very next morning, agreeing that we would use every stick of wood on the ground and find a new place for it somewhere in the garden. In the next two weeks, long, rounded boughs became a bower and a sweet little bench where a climbing rose would go; the entryway was a graceful arbor made from curved uprights and long, bendable whips. All the twisted limbs went into the fence. We wove the long, flexible twigs across it like a wattle basket, and with all the leftover scraps we made a quirky trellis.

We had the best time! What had been an unremarkable strip of crabgrass lawn was transformed into a magical fairyland composed of what already was there. Even my grief for my mother's life and death was an essential ingredient, for only in my extremity of sorrow would I have considered taking on the job of pulling up all that crabgrass. It had been my grieving, my therapy, and my offering to her.

The garden features Pete and I added, however, were less tangible; they represented our unfettered imaginations let loose in this small space. They represented all that was fun about the project, and in one another we had each found a talented work buddy. It was an unforgettable collaboration. Pete wondered if he shouldn't pay me for the privilege of working on my garden, and for my part, I wondered if all we ever needed to achieve anything in this world was a good idea, imagination, and a friend.

Once the structure had taken shape, I was ready to see leafy greens and flowering fruits in every corner, but winter was looming in California—our season of rain and wind and what we like to think of as "cold"—and the ground was brown dirt and dry as a bone. Patience not being my strong suit, I turned my attention to mulch. Everywhere I went, I begged other people's fall throwaways: their autumn leaves and dirty straw were my humus. Horse manure and kitchen compost, wood chips and rabbit poop were welcome gifts from bemused friends glad to get rid of it. Worms and mushroom spores, banana peels and torn-up cardboard all became layers in my garden that, while garbage right now, would become fluffy loam in the spring. I could hardly wait.

Once spring was in the offing, a gardener friend offered me a bag of cover-crop seeds—fava beans, vetch, and clover, all nitrogen fixers. I broadcast them proudly on my small field of aspiring soil. Like a nervous new mother, I examined the garden every day for green sprouts, and when they did finally come popping up out of their mulchy bed, I could hardly believe my luck.

Spring comes early in our part of Northern California, and by the end of February our "green manure" waved in the wind. Favas grew tall and delicate vetch wound its way up their stems. Wild radish plants put out prickly leaves. The small round leaves of nasturtium caught droplets of morning dew. No flowers yet, but the promise of gifts to come. Voracious snails and red worms and the first butterflies began making their appearance and growing fat on the land. Literally. Before spring was past, we had fava bean plants nine feet tall, which no farmer friends could account for, and cosmos flowers up to my shoulders. I figured that the healing prayers I had spread into the earth while pulling up all that crabgrass was the fertilizer that had made the difference.

During that first year of exuberant plant growth, I had the feeling that everything I needed to know could be learned from the garden: the patience required to wait for shoots to emerge out of the earth; the abundance and generosity when they did; the astonishing beauty of simple things; the ability to adjust to changing conditions and my occasional neglect. I watched small seeds put down delicate roots and, using what was freely given—sunshine, starlight, air, and rain—become sprawling tomato vines bursting with flowers and fruits. I saw the tiniest squash seedling—actually, a volunteer from the compost—threaten to take over the neighborhood and provide everyone's supper into the bargain. The most humble bit of green popping out of the ground could grow into a Mexican sunflower with velvety stalks and uncountable bright orange blossoms; a cutting of fennel from the hills could shoot up into feathery fronds as tall as a tree.

And when the season drew to an end, I watched my plants gracefully sink lower and lower towards the earth, letting go of their vividness, their power, and their seeds, while taking on a different kind of beauty and dying with no regrets. They were on to the next stage of their cycle. They knew what to do as they slumped onto the ground, giving their substance back to the earth for next year's growth.

The wisdom of my garden made me smile, and it had a similar effect on passersby. We live in the city, close to both a children's playground and a hospital, which means that many people walk by our house on their way to work, to the park, or to visit sick friends. Many are preoccupied and rushed, some are strolling, still others are toddlers with their parents or nannies. But all of them stop.

From inside the house, I watch them finger the fence, gaze at the flowers, point out things to their friends, and then walk away smiling. When I am out gardening, they ply me with questions and compliments, and we have conversations. I beckon the children in, inviting them to taste a peapod, a cherry tomato; to their parents, I often offer some herbs for dinner. I especially love meeting the children. I introduce them to the plants by smell, letting them do their own picking. At first they are shy, but the next time they pass by, they come in as if they own the place. I take this as a compliment.

Japan has a tradition of tea ladies, "invisible" women healers who place their tea stalls at crossroads where many people come by. As they serve tea, the tea ladies also provide a listening ear. It looks casual, and it is, but there is also a level of deliberate intention in their pouring of the tea, their receptive interest, their discreet empathy. These women make a point of being there on most days. They know that people will return to that crossroads, hoping to find her there when they are in distress and have a story to tell.

I am learning to be a tea lady in my garden.

Dance Healing

A FEW YEARS BEFORE I went to Brittany, I decided to finally fulfil my lifelong yearning to be a choreographer, and at the age of forty-one I became a dancer.

Getting my body back into shape after having three children wasn't so easy, but in the process of relaxing tight muscles, exercising stiff joints, and relearning my body's rhythms, I made a radical discovery: with every muscle release came a corresponding emotion, a memory of whatever had caused that muscle to contract in the first place. My body was a virtual archaeological dig of my past history. As I worked on loosening my spine, each bend and twist brought tears of ancient pain: my throat held sobs that had never come out, my toes cramped at memories of being too scared to run.

I became entranced—horrified, in fact—by the secrets my body had been keeping all these years. By the end of the first year of exploration, I was totally hooked on the process. Actually, I didn't have much choice because, having opened this Pandora's box of long-held emotion, my secrets would no longer stay hidden. If I did not allow them out, they let me know in no uncertain terms, then they would force their way out in the form of serious illness. I was lucky to have uncovered them in the nick of time.

My first task was to turn the garage at home into a makeshift studio. I cleared out accumulated junk, constructed a sprung wood floor of plywood and oak parquets, put skylights in the roof, and replaced the ageing garage doors with glass. I used the studio daily, trying out new dance techniques, martial arts, and improvisations, and I signed up for a class in choreography.

It was improvisation that I loved the best. Once again the hunter-gatherer, I studied briefly with every kind of teacher in town, then came back to my home studio to play with what I had learned. Over time, my experimentations evolved into a personal technique based upon an extended, improvised warm-up. It resulted in a relaxed, focused mind and body, a state that was very much like meditation. My muscles would be loose and warm, my breathing deep and even, and my mind receptive and creative. Anything was possible in that state; I was flexible, calm, and attentive. I had never felt happier. From there, the hard work of uncovering unconscious material could proceed unimpeded.

Working without mirrors—with my eyes closed, in fact—my mind opened up, along with my body and my heart. Hours in the studio passed like minutes. This practice was a lifeline to my authentic self, as my limbs grew strong and supple and my spine, released like a snake into running water, learned again how to bend freely. With each new release of tight muscles, emotional memory was brought up into consciousness and my history poured forth. Sorrow and anger came out; old traumas rose to the surface, where I could take a good look at them and then let them go. Forgiveness came easily now, along with the clarity of grief, where I had otherwise placed blame. I dared to feel love, where I had long assumed hate. I felt places soften that had long ago grown hard.

My voice opened up, too. What had been a short range of one squeaky octave became a sweep of notes—booming bass to clear, high soprano. I had no idea where this remarkable voice was coming from; certainly, it came *through* me, rather than *from* me. In the beginning, I would start to weep as soon as I opened my mouth to sing, but as each bout of crying loosened my throat a little bit more, the sounds gradually sounded more like music.

It was like I was becoming a new lover to myself, discovering each part of this body by close and fascinated touching, bringing to life places that had not even known they were sleeping.

To be truthful, it often felt like self-inflicted agony because the process required so much painful honesty, not to mention screaming muscles, but in the end it was worth every hot minute of it. In no time at all, I was feeling better than I had in years. People commented on how well I looked. "What did you do?" they asked.

"Come into my studio and I'll show you," I replied. And thus began my healing work.

I loved my work and was thrilled that it was an art form—dance—that had led to the healing of my old wounds. The process of healing became an art form in itself. My body in motion became a metaphor for my life. Events from childhood would show up in my body as symbols of the human condition: my grandmother immobilized for a lifetime in a wheelchair was Stuckness and Lack of Balance; my mother slowly going mad was Shame of Silent Despair and Repressed Anger. My body had recorded it all. My child's responses to the tragedies in my family emerged from the depths of myself, as my body played out everybody's dramas. At every level—physical, emotional, psychological, spiritual, and finally, artistic—I danced my way through the history of my kin. Finally, I was left with mostly myself, free.

Improvisation was the key—improvisation and close attention to the sensations in my body. I learned how to relax my mind enough to feel what was there, letting my body's imagination roam free without censure. A lift of the arm might lead to a swooping turn, which I would follow around the studio until the momentum swung my head right, then left, followed by a sharp throbbing in the area of my shoulder blade. This might suggest a subtle exploration of my upper spine and back. From there might come rotations of both shoulders, which would move my wrists and arms in a dance of their own.

Invariably, emotion would follow the movement: a child crying behind a locked door; wasting bodies in wheelchairs and the stench of urine; desperation dimly witnessed. Stories played themselves out, sometimes with words and colors, sometimes not, like dreams being told while they were being dreamed, often with insights popping like flashing lights, linking the images to current issues in my life. I would hold onto them like precious jewels, letting them sink in slowly.

Day after day I plumbed the depths of my own past, following knots in my own body to where the emotions resided down at the edges of awareness. Gradually, it seemed to require less effort. My movements became silky and smooth, following the path of least resistance with an ease I had never known before. I was becoming the dancer I had always longed to be, and dance pieces emerging from this work of healing were good enough to perform.

I created a small dance company and, for two seasons, did just that, surprising myself by being successful at it. I had become not only a dancer but also a choreographer. Yet, after all was said and done, it was the healing work that called more strongly. I shifted my attention back to the body itself and movement as a vehicle for transformation.

As I became more adept at finding that blessed state of relaxed concentration through the warm-up, and being able to identify and release places in the body where the natural flow of energy was blocked, it became increasingly evident to me that I had stumbled upon a spiritual as well as a healing practice. It was a state of grace I had discovered—a grace that did not need to be sought in any exotic traditions but was already right here in our own bodies. It was our birthright, and all we needed to do was remove the emotional blocks that obscured it. No doubt it was easier said than done, but the Holy Grail was quite within our reach when we had the will to put in the effort.

People began coming. Together, we danced the warm-up until we were in a state of relaxed concentration, then identified the congested energy in our bodies. For the next hour or so, as we danced, we paid close attention to how we felt and what came up into consciousness. I danced along, watching their bodies and expressions and feeling the energy in the studio. I was a companion in their process, a guide rather than a healer; we were students and teachers together. I provided the structure and the space; the person used the opportunity to do the work of self-healing, with me as witness.

It was an important realization that, after all is said and done, none of us can heal anybody but ourselves. What I could do was teach what I had learned and take the journey with others, bearing witness and sharing pain. Our deepest shames could then become a kind of compost, exposed and shaped until they glowed like diamonds under pressure. Some of the most vivid theater I have ever witnessed was in my studio during those years. There was so much mutual trust that people were willing to reveal the angst of their darkest shadows, create beauty from them, and transform pain into works of art. Together, we faced every fear—even death itself—and emerged exhausted but whole.

There is authentic beauty in the freedom of our bodies moving through space: beauty itself seems to be the healing force. As we move with grace and body wisdom, impotence is replaced by strength and self-knowledge. The body never lies. The self-hate that so many of us take for granted shows itself immediately, but as we become conscious of our unconscious gestures, we release the grip of shame and self-loathing, and eventually we wonder how we could have been so mistaken. Bit by bit, our arms reach out, legs spring in a leap, and we find ourselves dancing with ease and freedom—whole, healthy, Holy.

Healing with Sound

The Universe emanates from one completely subtle sound
that gives rise to all the other vibrations...
This throbbing vibration moves into the atmosphere like a resonance,
and from the interplay of its vibrations,
a symphony of energies comes forth...
The whole Universe is the result of the proliferation
of these vibrations emanating from the Primal Sound—
the subtle sound that arises at a frequency before noise.

—CREATION HYMN OF THE
KASHMIRI HINDU SHAIVITES

MORE THAN 2,500 YEARS AGO, the Greek philosopher Pythagoras defined stone as "frozen music." We now understand this literally to be the case, as modern science has shown that every particle in the physical Universe takes its characteristics from the pitch, pattern, and overtones of its particular frequency—its song. This is true of every force, every thought, every motion in the world. In essence, before we make music, music makes us. Music provides the pattern; the way music works is how everything works. The deep structure of music is the same as the deep structure of everything else.

This makes intuitive sense to me. Reading in the wisdom traditions of many ancient cultures, I find echoes of the same idea everywhere I look:

The Lakota Sioux sing this chant:

All creatures alive are Mother Earth's songs;
All creatures that die are Mother Earth's songs;
The winds blowing by are Mother Earth's songs;
And she wants you to sing all her songs.

Among the Australian Aborigines, the wise man is "he who knows many songs." The ancient Egyptian god Osiris chants:

I come forth by day singing;
I am born of sky, filled with light.

From the Zohar, the Hebrew mystical text:

Angels are made from God's breath to sing his glory.

And when I was at the stones in Brittany, I received my own version of the same teaching: *Just sing.*

Until that magical evening of my improvised duet with Jiri by the sea, when the song seemed to be singing us and the world was simple, clear and rapturous, I had no idea what *just sing* actually meant. I got a glimpse that night, when all we had really done was to let go into the freedom of our own voices singing. Actually, as I recall our little two-step at the edge of the surf, it was more like "being sung" than actively singing. It was as if we were bells being rung, as if we had been taken over by the song coming through us. I will never forget the pleasure, the sacramental feel of that evening and its intimation of eternity.

It never ceases to amaze me that such pleasure has the power to heal, but it does, unfailingly. I have observed it again and again.

A visit to the Big Island of Hawaii, where the newest vent in the eastern flank of Kilauea Volcano—Pu'u O'o—was in its early eruptive phase, was one such occasion.

My husband and I had hiked to one edge of the live flow as dusk was coming on, to watch new land being formed. Rivers of moving fire were pouring slowly across old lava beds toward the sea, clearly visible in the darkening sky. We had followed the others toward the volcano's moving edge, to where the flow slowed and thinned before finally crusting over, trapping the last layer of red-hot molten lava beneath black crust—new rock.

The others drifted away, flashlights bobbing in the dark, and we stayed behind to watch the molten stuff sizzle, turn from red to black and harden where we stood. Before I knew it was happening, I found myself singing.

Just sing.

Sounds bubbled up from deep in my belly, as if some ancient Hawaiian chant was using me to be sung. I had never heard sounds like these before, much less sung them, but my voice seemed to know what to do. I sang deep, repeated tones that reminded me of some very ancient chant that might once have been intoned in this place. The strong rhythm burst out of me and poured into the shimmering night air.

The place where we stood at the edge of the flow was searingly hot, and while I was singing little cracks began appearing in the black crust, letting through spurts of the red-hot stuff underneath. It poured out a short way, slowed, and again crusted over. Curious, I directed my voice to the new crust; again, little fissures appeared, red and hot, and more molten rock spurted forth.

"See that?" I called excitedly to my husband, who had backed off from the searing heat of the flow's edge.

"Sure do," he confirmed, as I moved to another, untested spot and focused my voice on an edge of curled crust. Again, the new black rock opened up and sent forth a spurt of red-hot lava. Wherever I stood, whatever I chanted, the molten rock seemed to be responding to the sound of my voice. For me, this was a radical discovery! On the hike back to the coast, I kept looking back and exclaiming, until I tripped and fell hard, scraping my leg badly enough to have to spend the next two days swathed in bandages and stuck in a chair.

But it had confirmed for me that sound and intention could move matter. If my voice improvising Hawaiian chants could make molten rock shift and split open, might not singing do something similar to the human body and help it heal?

In the eighteenth century, a German scientist named Ernst Chladni vibrated a sand-covered metal plate with a violin bow, and discovered that the agitated sand eventually settled into a mandala-like pattern of great symmetry and beauty. Two centuries later, in the 1960s, the Swiss natural scientist Hans Jenny created what he called a *tonoscope,* an instrument with plates and membranes, and took the experiments even farther. He vibrated his instrument with violin bows, with his voice singing through cardboard tubes, with recordings of classical symphonies. Upon the plates and membranes he placed a variety of substances—powders, metal filings, liquids—and photographed the substances responding to changing pitches, dynamics, and tempi.

And what patterns were created! When the pitch was low, the patterns were symmetrical and beautiful, but simple; when the pitch was raised, the substance rearranged itself into more complex patterns; and when a symphony was played on a phonograph, the matter positively danced. Sound apparently not only moved matter but created patterns of great beauty reminiscent of structures in the physical world.

If form and structure were ultimately created by sound, I reasoned, we ought to be able to change an unhealthy pattern in the physical body to a healthy one by finding the song—the frequencies and patterns of sound—that might approach the balanced Primal Sound and harmonize with it.

Isn't that essentially what indigenous healers who dance and chant themselves into trance are doing? By the use of traditional practices that put them into an altered state, they reach a "felt state" of mystical participation with the All, and in the rapture of that connection, transmit the healing power of the Universe to those who are ill.

I know such practices still exist in the United States—not only among indigenous people but right here in the city. For years, I sang in a gospel choir in an African-American church and experienced this kind of ecstatic *participation mystique*. It helped heal me. And I watched it heal others in the congregation, time and again, as people in despair were lifted up by the power of the choir rocking and singing, raising the rafters until the very air was changed. Nobody questioned that it worked, and all of our lives were helped by it.

The opposite is true, as well: discordant, soulless noise that entrains the body away from a healthy balance of frequencies, destroys. Remember Joshua and the Battle of Jericho? The reason that I am as intimate as I am with the power of sound is that I once lived near an ongoing construction site, and for a long time I tried to shut out the noise by simply ignoring it. Then, one day I went over the edge and had to be hospitalized. My adrenal glands, depleted from such a long time of sending out adrenalin, finally quit and I collapsed. It took a while to recover. Now I avoid exposure to noise to the extent that I can, but I wonder if all of us who live in noisy cities do not suffer from a similar depletion?

Here is how I work with someone who is ill, using movement to raise my own vibrations into an altered, or shamanic, state, then allowing myself to *just sing* to the person. I begin by warming up my body; this relaxes my musculature, allows my breathing to become deep and even and my mind free of thoughts. Next, I ask for health and wholeness for both of us. Then, I listen.

Invariably, sounds appears in my mind's ear and, when they ring true to me, I sing what I *hear* out loud, following it wherever the song leads. The song that spins out from that first sound is always new, always unexpected, and invariably tells me something about the person's problem. While I give the song my full attention, the quality of that attention is as relaxed and easy as swinging in a hammock in the sun. Once I feel that depth of relaxation, I know I can trust what comes next, that whatever comes through is what the person needs. By the time the song draws to its inevitable end, my body is throbbing with coursing energy and I am hot and happy. In the delicious silence that follows, I transmit the energy to the person on the mat before me.

Love is the emotion; sound is the vehicle; healing is the intention.

It's not hard to do. Anybody can learn how. Imagine if we all sang to each other when we got sick; can you see every house and street ringing with our songs? This could be the cutting edge of the new medicine!

One evening, after a rousing choir rehearsal, I wrote this update of Psalm 150:

Sing praise for all that is:

Extending everywhere endlessly
through Space and through Time.

Sing praise to the farthest outward reaches of the Cosmos
and to the subtlest inner reaches of Being.

Sing praise to the Galaxies,
With suns and stars and roving planets.

Sing praise to the miracle of matter and life,
To the dense rocks and waters,
To rooted green plants,
To earthbound creatures and winged ones,
To the tiny vastnesses in every atom.

Praise the Grand Universe
With harps and timbrels and flutes;
Praise all existence
With Congas and Gamelans,
Kotos and Gospel choirs.
Give praise with Reggae and Symphonies,
Oratorios and Flamenco guitars;
Strum strings and pipe on pennywhistles,
Strike up the band and let the trombones wail.

Belt out praise with Grand Opera,
Steel bands, Jazz and Blues.
Ring the bells and blow the bagpipes.
Beat the drums and sound the trumpets.

Let everything that has voice
Sing out praise.
To the end of the breath, Sing!
With every single cell, Sing!
Body, mind and spirit, Sing!

15

Natasha

Ancestral Landscapes

WHEN I LEARNED how Carolyn had developed her healing powers at Carnac to process her family history through dance and sound, then went on to work with others using the same methods, I was reminded of the philosophy of one American Indian tribe. Someone who was ill would be asked:

"When did you stop dancing?"

In other words, what was it that once happened to traumatize your body, and so restricted and distorted its natural flow of energy that illness resulted? When did you stop dancing in tune with the rhythms of Creation? I also recalled a statement by the dancer and choreographer Marie Rambert who said:

> "Movement never lies; it is a barometer showing the state of the soul's weather."

It seems that our souls, as well as our bodies and the landscape, experience emotional weather conditions. That may be why flexibility of the mind is so important, for it lets us move with the changes that always occur in Nature. If we become fixed in our attitudes, we cannot evolve beyond our prejudices and preconceptions; we simply project our fixed attitudes onto a world that follows another rhythm, a different pattern.

In the chapter on her garden, Carolyn talks about the emotional and physical clearing work she needed to do after her mother died. The old tree was severely pruned; it had overwhelmed the garden, shading it out—an old tree that had a journey of its own to make, leaving behind a farewell gift of wood to be used creatively for other purposes, so that its energies could be transmuted.

Like so many others who have worked with gardens and the land, Carolyn recognized that everything one needs to know about how to live one's life can be got-

Le Ménec alignment

ten from the natural world. My own feeling, also, is that this is a significant message for us all. Many ancestral teachings—from the Celtic Druids to the American Indians to the Taoists—emphasize learning from the natural world. But we have to pay close attention and fully recognize that we are part of a greater plan.

This is what Tatanga Mani, an American Indian of the Stoney Tribe, said in a passage from his autobiography, quoted in T. C. McLuhan's book, *Touch the Earth:*

> Oh, yes, I went to the White Man's schools. I learned to read from schoolbooks, newspapers, and the Bible. But in time I found that these were not enough. Civilized people depend too much on man-made printed pages. I turn to the Great Spirit's book, which is the whole of his creation. You can read a big part of that book if you study Nature. You know, if you take all your books, lay them out under the sun, and let the snow and rain and insects work on them for a while, there will be nothing left. But the Great Spirit has provided you and me with an opportunity for study in Nature's university, the forests, the rivers, the mountains, and the animals which include us.

Those comments about civilization and our education system are as valid now as when they were made in the early part of the twentieth century. To the people of the past, the whole landscape, along with everything in Nature, was sacred, worthy of honor and respect. In these days, having exploited the greater part of the natural world, we are starting to fear the consequences. Our wish for dominance is causing profound problems for our species; destruction of the habitats for plant, animal, and human life; pollution of the seas and our atmosphere; and a deep and growing sense of isolation in human society.

Many young people are disillusioned and angry, as they find themselves lacking in any sense of being rooted within family and society, cut off from their birthright in the natural world. In their yearning, they often become hostile and are unable, or unwilling, to fit into the competitive society we have created in our cities. One might say they have become creatively disempowered.

Another American Indian author, Ohiyesa, has written:

> As a child I understood how to give; I have forgotten this grace since I became civilized. I lived the natural life, whereas I now live the artificial.

What have you learned from Nature? The voice from the megalith asked, then I heard this:

The human body and that of the Earth Mother, including animals, birds, and plants, are all made of the same stuff, the stuff from which the solar system was created. Everything comes from the Source and returns to Source through the transmutation of energies. Without the vibrations of human love, nothing can return to the Source of Divine Love until it is healed by that human love.

In an inharmonious environment, only inspired humans can be harmonious within themselves, and that inspiration comes first from the love and warmth of personal relationships. If human relationships do not nourish the inner landscape, then the outer landscape often becomes bleak, too. Then it is not easy to find inner quiet or sacred space within yourself.

Without a conscious connection with the cosmic rhythms, many people feel that life is meaningless. There is, of course, always a subconscious connection with the celestial influences at work in your life, but when that remains unconscious it does not empower you, nor cause you to feel that you are actually a part of a Whole.

Your thought forms and your understanding contribute to the quality of your life. A long time ago when the whole planet was a Garden, people danced at sacred sites, celebrating the cycles of the seasons and their own rites of passage. They knew that the dance of life that flowed through them flowed also through the whole Universe.

Menhir at Narbon

It is the essential love of the Earth for the Cosmos, a dynamic union of Spirit and Matter that makes possible the transformation of energy at the sacred sites. Located all over the planet, many of these focal points are marked by the megaliths of the unknown peoples who were our forebears.

The word Love occurs repeatedly in the dialogue given to us by these Voices out of Stone, sounding with a loving resonance. We felt this same resonance in their presence, this higher-than-human love that may also be the highest vibration of Light. If only our medical researchers would study it more closely! The transformative power of Love as it flows through the body of the Earth and all living species is the essence of healing, and it can effectively restore balance both in us and in our environment.

Love is possibly the ultimate source of energy from which all other energies are expressed. It cannot be manufactured or patented; it can only be given and received. Each of us, working to learn from our personal histories, is on a journey toward a state of grace that exists and may be tapped. To do that, we have to find the key in our own hearts to unlocking and discovering for ourselves the sense of belonging to the Universe.

In their understanding of their place in the Universe, many American Indian beliefs were similar to those of the megalith builders. Ohiyesa, born in 1862, said that his people, the Dakota, possessed remarkable powers of concentration and abstraction, and that their nearness to Nature kept the spirit sensitive to impressions not commonly felt and in touch with unseen powers. Chief Luther Standing Bear, born seven years later, said that man's heart, away from Nature, becomes hard.

Since becoming aware of the awesome power of the sacred landscape we inherit from our ancestors, I have felt certain that there once *was* a time on this beautiful planet of Earth, many hundreds of thousands of years ago, when people lived by the law of Love. Organized religion would have been unnecessary, as people then understood that the source of humanity and every form of life was Celestial Love and that all life on Earth was an expression of that Love. To such people all life would have been sacred, as would have been the entire landscape, of which they knew themselves to be an integral part. Who knows but that in those distant days, our ancestors may have been able to live in a continuous state of ecstasy?

Archaeologists are increasingly uncovering traces of mankind's history that extend farther and farther into the past. They have found evidence of sophistication in civilizations long since gone and proof of a well-developed science of mathematics and a detailed knowledge of astronomy. The farther back they look, the more they find indications that the peoples of old were not warlike. Excavation of the remains at various burial places has shown that there was a long history of extending equal importance to women and men. Weapons and stone tools were made simply for hunting, fishing, and household tasks. Territory does not seem to have been a matter for dispute. Certainly, there were few defensive sites until settled agriculture became widespread. The tribal wars that still plague us today seem not to have developed much before the increase in population that followed the discovery and use of metal in the Age of Copper.

In the Carnac area of France, near Belz, an untouched megalithic site has recently been found, just as it was about to be bulldozed for a housing development. When fully excavated, it seems very likely to provide more detailed information about the daily life of the neolithic period.

La Menga, Spain

In Spain, not far from Malaga, the well-known site of Antequera has three large and well-preserved dolmens of massive, shaped stonework. Dated to around 2,500 B.C., they are set in an extraordinary landscape. The largest is the dolmen of Menga, built over a deep interior well. It faces the sunrise, across the plain, angled toward a curious mountain that resembles the head of an Indian chief lying on his back looking up at the sky—a noble and quite breathtaking profile. From inside the dolmen, looking toward the entrance, his head can be seen beautifully silhouetted against the sky. Clearly, that is just one part of an essentially sacred landscape, recognized from an even earlier time.

In southeastern Turkey, the extensive site called Göbekli Tepe has been under excavation for some years. Amazingly, it is dated to around eleven thousand years ago, or about six thousand years earlier than the circular earthen ring of Stonehenge. So far, four oval structures have been revealed, and it is likely there are a number of others. They are considered to be stone-built shrines and have a number of T-shaped pillars, five meters tall, spaced around the enclosing wall. Many of those large stone slabs are elaborately decorated with carvings in relief of animals and birds. The alignment to the cardinal points of the compass suggests that solar observations took place there, at a time well before farming and settlement in the area had replaced nomadic hunting.

The whole complex has been preserved because it was abandoned after about a thousand years of use and deliberately covered over with earth. Until the discovery of this extraordinary place, the six-thousand-year-old Nabta circle in the Egyptian desert, with its five stone rows and three-meter megaliths, was considered to be the oldest astronomically aligned monument. It is often forgotten that the earliest known beginnings of Stonehenge are the massive timber postholes that have been dated to between 7,000 and 8,000 B.C.; now, Göbekli Tepe takes us farther back.

At Laetoli in northern Tanzania, Mary Leakey led a 1978 expedition that discovered the fossil footprints of three walking humans.* Incredibly, they were made between 3.6 and 3.8 million years ago. Stone mortars, pestles, and obsidian tools, found during nineteenth-century gold-mining in the gravel of an old riverbed deep under Table Mountain in California, may be no less than 33 million years old from the geological strata in which they were embedded, although archaeologists do not agree on the authenticity of the find. True or not, extraordinary archaeological findings, and others that continually come to light, all help us to reassess our ancient heritage and see just how much we still have to learn about the past and, more importantly, from it.

What, for example, are we to make of the fact that some two thousand years before Plato's birth people were evidently aware of the five Platonic solids, each of which can, by definition, fit within a sphere, the shape of perfection? That knowledge of three-dimensional geometry is demonstrated by a number of granite balls found in Scotland, clearly sculpted to represent those five solid forms for unknown mathematical or other purposes.

Historians are still wedded to the idea of a steady progression from the primitive human to our present level of sophistication; yet, it appears that the period of

---

* See *Ancient Traces: Mysteries in Ancient and Early History* by Michael Baigent (London: Penguin Books, 1999).

the megaliths was not the beginning but may, rather, have signaled the end of an era of some earlier, highly developed civilization, which might itself have spent thousands of years in a gradual decline.

The megalithic culture, with its many variations in style and type of stone, extended right across the world for several thousand years, a period of adventurous ocean travel long before America was reached by the Egyptians and Phoenicians, whose inscriptions remain there,* or the Southern Hemisphere was explored and mapped by the medieval Chinese. During all that time, there was clearly a deep and detailed knowledge of movements in the Heavens, in relation to navigation and earthly life—and an attunement to them by the practice of Earth rites from an even earlier period.

Information of this kind is recorded in cuneiform writing on clay tablets from the Sumerian and Babylonian era, large numbers of which languish in the basements of most major museums. They include many astronomical observations and advanced mathematics. Sumerian calculations were *sexagesimal*, based on alternate multiplication by the numbers 6 and 10, a more advanced and flexible system than our decimal system, which is simply based on the number 10. Sumerian numerics give us the 60 that we still use for counting seconds and minutes of time, for the seconds and 360 degrees of a circle, for the measurement of global latitude and longitude, even for our 12-hour days and nights.

Their inscribed tablets indicate that arithmetic, for them, did not start as ours does with the number 1, but with 12,960,000, which could then be divided downward by using fractions. That curiously high number is 3,600 squared, and—as Zecharia Sitchin says in *Genesis Revisited*—is literally "astronomical," for it is exactly 500 times the 25,920-year cycle of the Precession of the Equinoxes.

Precession refers to the wobble of the Earth's axis, which, during that extremely long period, completes a circle around the twelve constellations of the zodiac, taking 2,160 years to pass from one house, or Age, to the next, moving back by one degree every 72 years.

At present, we are moving from the Age of Pisces into the Age of Aquarius. The number 72, the numbers 12 (one sixth of 72), and 144 (twice 72), occur frequently in the Bible, as well as in myths and stories of many other traditions. These numbers also occur in the dimensions and the longitudinal spacing of some of the major megalithic monuments around the world. We wonder, how did the Sumerians know about precession so precisely? And when was it discovered? The celestial

* See *America B.C.: Ancient Settlers in the New World* by Barry Fell (New York: Pocket Books, 1989).

observations and prolonged record-keeping required to establish such a vast cycle would have taken the lifetimes of many astronomers, a process that seems highly improbable.

Those same precessional numbers are found in the somewhat later Mayan calendar, in which a Baktun is 144,000 days. Thirteen Baktuns make up a full cycle, the current one being due to end on December 22, 2012. These numbers are also the basis of the ancient Hindu cycles of world civilizations, the four endlessly repeating Yugas of birth, growth, maturity, and decay. We are in the fourth, the Kali-Yuga, or period of decline, which lasts for 432,000 years (72 times 6,000) and, we should note, is marked by wars and increasing social disturbance.

No system of numbers earlier than that of Sumer is recorded. Their advanced knowledge of astronomy and mathematics must have emanated from another, earlier source. Some believe it could have come from the Annunaki of the Sumerian writings, the Nefilim or sons of God in the Book of Genesis. Some think it may have come from the incomers known as the Shining Ones, those who, we are told in the earliest creation stories, came from another planet and brought us knowledge, then interbred with our indigenous ancestors to create modern mankind.

Unfortunately, archaeology is as resistant to a change of perspective as all other orthodox science, and for the same reasons. It would mean rewriting the textbooks, jobs would be lost, and previous assumptions would have to be reassessed in the light of new research. Yet a growing amount of evidence points to mankind's life on Earth as being older, far older, and much better informed than we have previously thought.

We must not forget that Sumer eventually destroyed itself by cutting down the vast cedar forests of Lebanon and Syria for fuel, which reduced the rainfall, caused salinity in the groundwater, and led eventually to the loss of the irrigated land downstream that for so long had supplied food for a growing population. The Greeks did the same in classical times, leaving a barren landscape; they were followed by the Romans in Italy, who cut down their trees for fuel and metal smelting, then had to conquer North Africa to find fertile land from which to import the grain they needed. Each civilization has exhausted the energy source of its time and collapsed—as we are in imminent danger of doing now, in our relentless exploitation of the limited resource of oil for power generation and transport.

While a great deal of essential knowledge has been lost over the millennia, and present events are not encouraging, we are learning in many ways to open our hearts to the power of Love. If we can recover the knowledge of our ancestors maybe this time, we can make wiser use of it.

16

Carolyn

Science and Spirit

DURING THOSE MONTHS of singing to my husband during his radiation treatments, the insights I received were like a curriculum in the interface between science and spirit. I was led from understanding how family history influenced our current states of health to ever more subtle information: about how energy clusters and creates matter and form; about how the consciousness of the Universe is transformed, from subtlest to most dense, until living bodies can receive it via their DNA. I recognized that I was receiving information of great import and that I should pay close attention.

After each session, I would excitedly recount the new material to my husband, trying to find language to express these ephemeral, multidimensional insights I was receiving about the interface between the subtle world and the concerns of science. He would listen with curiosity, but his response was invariably some version of, "Well, it's interesting, but it's not Science."

Once, he muttered, "Sounds more like religion to me." His tone was less than objective, and I was hurt.

It reminded me of one winter day, several years earlier, when we had had a mystifying adventure among the Ancestral Pueblo, once called Anasazi, ruins of Chaco Culture National Historical Park in New Mexico. We had gone to Chaco on the first anniversary of my sister's death to honor her request that I go to the place she loved the best in the world. I was to climb up alone to the ruins of Mesa Alta, which she had always been too scared to climb, while my husband stayed below in the canyon. Our prayers would then go out simultaneously from above and below. We synchronized our watches and planned to meet up again at the trailhead in exactly two hours.

When I was ready to come back down two hours later, I saw him waiting by the ruins at the bottom of the trail, but when I reached the canyon floor he was gone. I called, and my voice echoed off canyon walls. For two frightening hours I scoured the ruins on the canyon floor, in every direction, finding no trace of the most reliable man I have ever known. Fearing the worst, I ran to the road to jog the three miles toward the visitor center. Night was coming on fast. It was freezing there in the dark canyon, and help was miles away. I was terrified.

The moment I left the environs of the ruin he suddenly materialized, as if out of thin air. He was at least as frantic as me.

"Where were you?" we both yelled.

"Right here!" we both insisted.

"But, but... !" we both exclaimed.

Our stories, which we told each other over and over, were the same: we had seen each other when I started down the trail, but then we weren't there. He had waited and waited, walked around for two hours, called me again and again, and finally decided to go get help at the visitor center. I told him I had done exactly the same thing—but it made no sense.

Could we have continually been somehow out of earshot of each other? Could we really have continually been turning the very corner that would put us out of each other's range of vision? The area at the base of the mesa is cluttered but not all that large.

Two hours of searching in the same place without finding each other seemed impossible—unless we had somehow entered different dimensions. This was a déjà vu of that time with Jiri at the dolmen in the woods at Moustoir-Ac. Chaco, after all, is a very mysterious place, and there is much about the Ancestral Puebloan people that scholars have never been able to explain. To my scientist husband, mutual invisibility was impossible. Things like that did not happen.

That was several years ago; we still do not have a satisfactory explanation that both of us can accept of what happened that day.

Until our Chaco Canyon debacle, I had never been able to grasp why our communications always bogged down when we talked about what was "real." I tended to find his scientific views too limiting for me, and he considered my insistence upon a wider view too judgmental of him. On that cold winter evening, driving down the long canyon road, as we recounted to each other the experience of our misadventure, I finally accepted the fact that my husband and I perceived the world through different lenses. I also realized that neither of us was wrong; we just saw a different world.

To him, "the world" meant "the physical world," a place of form and life, forces and elements, chemicals and astronomical bodies, in ultimately measurable Space. Humans and their instruments could objectively examine the smallest particles to the farthest galaxies. What was outside the realm of observable reality was not of scientific interest.

To me, "the world" was boundless, a Universe of multiple interlocking systems of dynamic, intelligent energy on a continuum from invisible to visible and beyond, which emerges continuously from a whole, unified matrix of energy—perhaps what scientists now call *dark energy*. What our human senses perceived as *physical* was a part, but not all, of a many-dimensioned reality, without which there would be no material world as we know it. To me it made no sense to study the material world without acknowledging this intelligent, energetic field from which it emerged. The larger context was essential to understanding our world. I was adamant on this point.

So was he.

For me, the fact that he and I had been invisible to each other in the vicinity of the ruin for over two hours was a rare but entirely possible phenomenon. Who knew what technologies these ancient peoples possessed? Whoever they were, hadn't they managed to construct an extensive city of stone structures in the canyon long before the mechanical era? Didn't their artifacts show that they understood complex moon cycles as well as transits of the sun; that they could build a lasting system of roads that stretched straight as arrows for miles across canyons and mesas?

For him, convinced as he was that a description of the world could not include hidden dimensions right where he was standing, what had happened to us was "impossible." But, as I reminded him more than once, it had happened anyway. For that, he had no answer.

And there is the impasse between science and spirit: one viewpoint entertains only the possibilities that fit a material structure of the world, the other entertains possibilities that include the mystery of the invisible and unknown—and, no doubt, the unknowable as well.

"Reason cannot be the only one way of knowing," I have often argued, "and it's not even the best way!" I stomp around the house muttering about closed-minded scientists. Then he argues back,

"Then prove it!" and I retort in a louder voice, "You disprove it!"

I wonder, though, why people need to have this argument at all? It seems clear that all of us, the rationalists and the intuitives, are each simply talking about different ways of looking at the same Universe. We are wearing a different set of spectacles, that's all, and are aware of complementary aspects of the same Whole. The world is intrinsically both/and; it is only a limitation of our cultures' mindsets that insists upon things being either/or.

Like the blind men and the elephant, we define the world according to the part of the beast we know the best, but the elephant is more than just the tail or the trunk or the legs. By insisting upon one version of the truth, we are missing the diversity of the whole, wondrous miracle and are making our lives the poorer for it.

Something not well known about Sir Isaac Newton, whose mechanistic theory of the Universe has been the underpinning of western science for the past three hundred years, is that he was also a mystic. His understanding was that the vital force underlying the Universe was the basis for the magnificent clockwork of the mechanistic world, and that a true science investigated both the physical *and* the metaphysical to understand the extraordinary breadth of God's plan. He studied ancient Hermetical texts; he read Plato and Pythagoras; he practiced alchemy. He posited that the physical world was a reflection of the divine Source, in which everything was held in dynamic, interconnected, mutually responsive balance with everything else. To him, the world was alive and intelligent.

The Church of England suppressed this information, however, nor did the scientific establishment of the time take kindly to it. It appears that after having a nervous breakdown, Newton revised his theories to conform to social pressure. His personal mission had been to put together the seen and the unseen in a single, grand theory and present it to the public. But although he wrote volumes on the subject—both in Latin and in code—the pressure eventually caused him to back down and present only his expurgated research.

One can only wonder about the agonies he must have endured and how our culture might be different now had his whole vision been received by his peers. As it happened, after his work was published he had another nervous breakdown.

I look forward to a time when scientists and mystics can sit at the same table and work together on the current issues facing our society: energy, medicine, education, economics. What won't we be able to dream up together? I expect we will discover ways to access unlimited energy from the unified field so that, without the political horrors and pollution involved in fossil fuels, all people everywhere will be inexpensively illumined, cooled and warmed, and transported with ease.

I imagine us practicing healing techniques that use sound and touch, as well as drugs and radiation. I envision our children being taught reverence, as well as spelling and arithmetic, and learning that the intuition is as powerful as the intellect. I see our economies treating the resources of the natural world as gifts to be stewarded with care, recognizing that without the support of the Earth none of us would be here.

Early in his career, Albert Einstein said, "My goal in life is to read the mind of God," And later, toward the end of his life, he was said to have cried out, "I have run out of mathematics!"

And still physicists are searching for a field, a dark energy, a matrix that encompasses everything. Perhaps it is right here, right now, right where we're standing, waiting to be recognized by our hearts and spirits, as well as our minds.

Several years ago, I found myself up in the air over Arizona's Sonoran Desert with my friend Adriel Heisey, who was piloting his Ultralight with one knee so both hands would be free to photograph the land below—vivid palo verde trees in bloom, erosion patterns in the landscape, solitary Picacho Peak seen from above. We had taken off in the predawn dark of a spring morning on an exploring adventure and sat exposed in an open cockpit just in front of the wings, engine noise drowning out all sound, communicating through little speakers wired into earphones on our helmets. Adriel pointed out rock formations and the shapes of light, as the sun threw its first colors onto the edge of the desert.

I loved this man—loved who he was, his grand vision, the gentle quality of his heart. Being up in the air with him and seeing the world as he perceived it, was one of those rare gifts we are sometimes given if we are very lucky. Later, when the sun had erased most of the morning colors, he landed the plane and drove his truck to the base of Picacho Peak for a hike up to the rim—the same mountain we had just flown over. Carrying sandwiches in our backpacks, we walked up the switchbacks, talking. At one point, following him up and over a boulder in the trail, I heard myself exclaim, "Thank God you're in the world at the same time I am!"

It's that kind of moment I live for—when I have observed the world from above, from below, from within, with a beloved and am so filled I could burst with the joy of it. He and I knew this mountain's shape and geology and the life cycles of its spiny plant life, its resident birds and reptiles and insects. We walked its flanks and had flown in its airstreams through the clouds gathered above its summit. On that day, we were intimately part of Picacho and each other; we were related.

Call it a religious experience, call it a scientific fieldtrip… it doesn't matter. I loved it all—scuttling lizards, saguaro cacti, bristling sun, dry trail. For that day, we were part of the desert and one another: kin.

Indigenous peoples everywhere have long understood the intimacy of being part of a divine, coherent field, in which we are inextricably related to each other because we are woven from the same fabric. We can listen to their wisdom, remember that we all come from the same ecstatic field, and greet each other as the relatives we really are.

Mayan: *In Lak'ech,* I am another yourself.

Indian: *Namaste*, I bow to the God within you.

Egyptian: *Ua hua*, We are one.

To all our relations, say the Lakota Sioux: *Omatakeosin,*

To all of our relations.

AFTERWORD

Hamilton

And it is now time for us to say
the few words we have to say
Because tomorrow our soul sets sail.
—GEORGE SEFERIS, Translation by Rex Warner

WE WERE AWAKENED by the knocking soon after daybreak. I ran downstairs—we were asleep in our old farmhouse in the Auvergne—but there was no one at the door; all was calm and silent. Then the knocks started again, two firm raps in succession, a summons we could not ignore. It was not the first manifestation in the house—certain earlier ones had been more sinister relics of its past history—but this was clearly a message we had to listen to and possibly act upon.

We reflected. Intuition came to our aid, and we realized we were being summoned to watch the rising of the sun. Of course! The mainspring of our existence, the energy source of all life, the light upon which we are dependent for growth. Watching that daily spectacle we came to see the importance of it, the constancy of that star at the center of the solar system. Twice more in later days, and only on bright mornings, those resolute knockings were repeated, confirming the message. Once again, it was an indication that entities from another realm can communicate with us for a purpose.

It put us in mind of other experiences—some mentioned in this book—of Angelic and Devic presences at the megaliths set up by our ancestors. They also had purpose, were aware that other parallel worlds exist, and could recognize the life-enhancing power of the energy lines on which are set all their circles, dolmens, and menhirs. Truly, they were children of the Universe and have left their marks for our benefit.

Yet today that awareness is lost. We are out of touch. Instead, greed for material things is rampant, unstable financial institutions and worldwide corporations dominate, our societies are insecure and violent, the contrast between rich and poor is extreme and growing, and we suffer from a system of food distribution that leads to obesity on the one hand and starvation on the other. Add to that, the problems resulting from population growth, the demand for energy, the diminishing supply of clean water, the over-exploitation of every natural resource on the planet, and it is clear that we have to make rapid and fundamental changes in our attitude toward Nature and each other.

Even as technology advances, our manner of living becomes daily more complicated and venal, less confident, less secure. We are in thrall to technology in so many ways, but it cannot, by itself, resolve the problems that seem likely to engulf us. Only the adoption of a simpler, fairer, more sustainable way of life can do that, and it can only come about locally, with the individual; it cannot be imposed.

Our governments, corporations, and institutions are incapable of such revolutionary change because their aim is basically survival. Measures to reduce energy consumption, to moderate climate change, to relieve poverty are unquestionably needed; however, they may well come to be regarded as a deliberate political distraction from the principal underlying difficulty: namely, that our present habits of life are unhealthy and unsustainable.

To effect the necessary changes, it will take a sufficient number of individuals at the grassroots level using their inherent power of intention to form a critical mass influential enough to affect all echelons of society. The intention must be to achieve a state of grace, Utopian as that may seem: greater loving-kindness, greater empathy with one other and with all other diverse living species, seen or unseen.

In other words, we require an ethical, spiritual attitude toward life—one that no longer puts mankind at the top of the proverbial Tree of Life but recognizes that humanity and the garden of our home planet are essentially a small part of an infinitely greater consciousness. For that process of change we can call upon the Angelic help that is always available to us, and which many of us may feel lies behind the present book's content and integrity.

If this book inspires you to move in that direction, or simply to dance or sing, it will have done its job; you can thank the authors later! And don't forget your sense of humor—you will probably need it on the way.

... joy in the whole Universe, its form, its beauty,
the feeling of their own belonging to it, being part of it.

—BORIS PASTERNAK, from *Doctor Zhivago,* a story of love.

Further Reading

Baigent, Michael: *Ancient Traces*, Penguin Books, London, 1999.
Baker, John: *Adventures of a 21st Century Dowser,* Quicksilver Publications, UK,2008.
Burl, Aubrey: *A Guide to the Stone Circles of Britain, Ireland and France,* Yale University Press, 2006.

Capra, Fritjof: *The Tao of Physics*, Fontana Paperbacks, London, 1983.
Carr-Gomm, Philip: *The Druid Way,* Element Books, Shaftesbury, Dorset, 1993.
Cope, Julian: *The Modern Antiquarian*, Thorsons, UK, 1998. *The Megalithic European*, Element Books, UK, 2004.
Cortens, Theolyn: *Discovering Angels*, Caer Sidi Publications, Oxfordshire, 1995. *Working with Angels*, Caer Sidi Publications, 1996.

Emoto, Masaru: *Love Thyself; the Message from Water III*, Hay House, Carlsbad, California, 2006.

Fell. Barry: *America B.C. - Ancient Settlers in the New World* - New York Times Book Co, 1976.
Findhorn Community: *The Findhorn Garden Story*, Findhorn Press, Findhorn, UK, 2008.

Guilaine, Jean: *Au Temps des Dolmens*, Editions Privat, Toulouse, France, 1998.

Hall, Alan: *Water, Electricity, and Health*, Hawthorn Press, UK, 1997.
Hawkes, Jacquetta: *Man and the Sun*, Cresset Press, London, 1976.
Hawkins, Gerald S.: *Beyond Stonehenge*, Harper and Row, New York, 1973
Heath, Robin: *Sun, Moon, and Stonehenge*, Blue Stone Press, Stoneridge, New York, 1998.

Laszlo, Ervin: *Science and the Akashic Field: An Integral Theory of Everything*, Inner Traditions, Vermont, 2004

Lutyens, Mary: *Krishnamurti - The Open Door* - John Murray, London, 1988.

Martineau, John: *A Little Book of Coincidence*, Wooden Books, Powys, Wales, 2002.

McLuhan, T. C: *Touch the Earth*, Abacus (Sphere Books), London, 1973.

Miller, Hamish, and Broadhurst, Paul: *The Sun and the Serpent,* Pendragon Press, Cornwall, UK, 2000; also *The Dance of the Dragon*, Pendragon Press, Cornwall, UK, 1990.

Michell, John: *The New View over Atlantis,* Harper and Row, San Francisco, 1969, 1983

Miller, Hamish, and Brailsford, Barry: *In Search of the Southern Serpent*, Penwith Press and StonePrint Press, UK and NZ, 2006.

Mohen, Jean-Pierre: *Standing Stones - Stonehenge, Carnac and the World of Megaliths* - Thames and Hudson, London, 1999.

Naddair, Kaledon: *Keltic Folk and Faerie Tales*, Rider Books (Century Hutchinson), London, 1987.

O'Brien, Christian and Barbara: *The Shining Ones*, Dianthus Publishing, Cirencester, England, 1997.

Paterson, Jacqueline Memory: *Tree Wisdom*, Thorsons, UK, 1996.

Sheldrake, Rupert: *The Presence of the Past - Morphic Resonance and the Habits of Nature* - Park Street Press (Inner Traditions), Vermont, USA, 1995.

Silva, Freddy: Secrets in the Fields: *The Science and Mysticism of Crop Circles*, Hampton Roads, Virginia, 2002

Skinner, Stephen: *Sacred Geometry*, Gaia Books (Octopus Publishing), London, 2006.

Steiner, Rudolf: *The Archangel Michael,* Anthroposophic Press, New York, 1994.

Thomas, Andy (editor): *An Introduction to Crop Circles*, Wessex Books, Salisbury, UK, 2003.

Ywahoo, Dhyani: *Voices of our Ancestors*, Shambhala Publications, Boston, Mass, 1987.